NATIVE CAROLINIANS
THE INDIANS OF NORTH CAROLINA

Theda Perdue and Christopher Arris Oakley

North Carolina Department of Cultural Resources
Office of Archives and History
Raleigh

NORTH CAROLINA DEPARTMENT OF CULTURAL RESOURCES
Susan W. Kluttz
Secretary

OFFICE OF ARCHIVES AND HISTORY
Kevin Cherry
Deputy Secretary

HISTORICAL PUBLICATIONS SECTION
Donna E. Kelly
Administrator

NATIVE CAROLINIANS

THE INDIANS OF NORTH CAROLINA

To Noel, William, and Jessica

CONTENTS

ILLUSTRATIONS

FOREWORD

For many years one of the most popular titles offered by the Historical Publications Section of the North Carolina Office of Archives and History was *Indians in North Carolina* by Stanley A. South. First published in 1959, that pamphlet, now out of print, sold more than 70,000 copies during the next quarter century. The appeal of the subject to schoolchildren, citizens of North Carolina, and tourists is apparent.

In keeping with the agency's longtime commitment to producing concise and factual booklets of sound scholarship on the state's history, the Historical Publications Section is pleased to publish a revised edition of *Native Carolinians: The Indians of North Carolina* by Theda Perdue and Christopher Arris Oakley. Dr. Perdue, currently the Atlanta Distinguished Professor of Southern Culture at the University of North Carolina, Chapel Hill, is a leading authority on Indian history. She previously taught at the University of Kentucky, Western Carolina University in Cullowhee, and at Clemson University. Her publications include *Slavery and the Evolution of Cherokee Society, 1540–1866*, published by the University of Tennessee Press in 1979, and *Cherokee Editor: The Writings of Elias Boudinot*, published by the same press in 1983. Dr. Perdue brings to her work an interdisciplinary perspective that draws on the most recent archaeological and anthropological research as well as on historical studies. Dr. Christopher Arris Oakley is an assistant professor of history at East Carolina University specializing in North Carolina Native American history. His publications include *Keeping the Circle: American Indian Identity in Eastern North Carolina, 1885–2004*, published by the University of Nebraska Press in 2005, as well as several articles in scholarly journals.

The Historical Publications Section wishes to thank the North Carolina Commission of Indian Affairs for its cooperation and assistance during the preparation of this booklet. Robert M. Topkins edited the original manuscript, researched the illustrations, wrote the cutlines, and saw the booklet through press. Stephena K. Williams prepared the manuscript on a word processor, and Sally A. Copenhaver assisted with the proofreading. For this revised reprint, Susan

Trimble created a new typeset version, and an index was prepared by the section administrator. Christopher Arris Oakley updated this edition from the one printed in 1985.

Donna E. Kelly, *Administrator*
Historical Publications Section

ACKNOWLEDGMENTS

Theda Perdue expresses her thanks to the following individuals for their assistance: Jeffrey J. Crow and Robert M. Topkins of the North Carolina Office of Archives and History; Danny Bell, formerly of the North Carolina Commission of Indian Affairs; Dianna Carlson and Patricia Hammond, formerly of Western Carolina University; George Frizzell and Anne Rogers of Western Carolina University; John Finger of the University of Tennessee; Genie DesMarteau of Clemson University; and Flora Walker, formerly of Clemson University.

Chris Oakley would like to acknowledge his M.A. and Ph.D. advisers, David La Vere of the University of North Carolina Wilmington and John Finger of the University of Tennessee.

Chapter 1

NATIVE AMERICA

In 1492 Christopher Columbus sailed west from Spain with the intention of reaching the Orient. Columbus and other Europeans did not know that two continents, North and South America, separated Europe from the Far East. When Columbus reached land, he mistakenly believed he had found India, the name Europeans commonly applied to the whole of Asia; and he called the people he met "Indios," which translates from Spanish to English as "Indians." Historians have subsequently credited Columbus (and other Europeans such as Leif Ericson or Amerigo Vespucci) with the discovery of the "New World." But what about the "Indians" Columbus encountered? Surely this was no "New World" to them. In fact, they had discovered the Americas thousands of years before Columbus set sail. Spreading throughout both continents, these earlier discoverers developed distinct cultural traditions that changed over time. Among them were the first Carolinians.

The exact origins of human settlement in the Americas remain unknown at the present time: archaeological and geological discoveries point to the migration of man from Asia to North America during the last stages of the Ice Age, which lasted for thousands of years. During this time there were warm periods when the ice, which formed large glaciers, partially melted. The weather then turned cold again and glaciers reappeared, significantly lowering the level of the ocean. Water receded entirely from shallow areas, and dry land appeared where oceans once had been. One of these shallow areas was the Bering Strait, which during warm periods separated Asia from North America. When ice formed, the waterway disappeared, creating a land bridge between the two continents. Bands of hunters from Asia crossed this land bridge and entered America. Exactly when this migration occurred is uncertain. Geologists, scientists who study the earth itself, have determined that lower ocean levels exposed the land bridge between 50,000 and 40,000 years ago and again between 28,000 and 10,000 years ago. For a long time, scholars believed that man came to the Americas only during the latter period, but the discovery of new sites and the more precise dating of others indicate that people very likely crossed the land bridge during the earlier period.

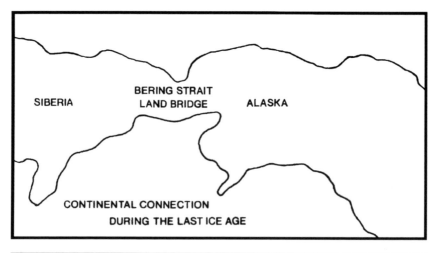

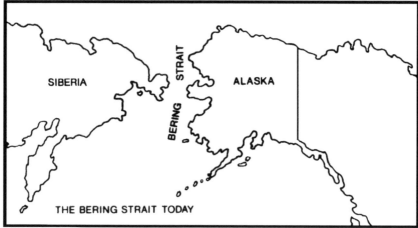

These maps depict the Bering Strait Land Bridge as it is believed to have existed during the latter stages of the Ice Age and the same area as it appears at the present time. The land bridge is believed by some scholars to have enabled man to migrate from Asia to North America. Maps from Jesse Burt and Robert B. Ferguson, *Indians of the Southeast: Then and Now* (Nashville and New York: Abingdon Press, 1973), 17.

These first Americans had no system of writing. Because most native peoples did not develop writing, they left no written records for historians to use in reconstructing their past. Historians must therefore rely upon the work of archaeologists, who study the material remains of cultures, for information about their history. Archaeologists are able to date some remains by using very sophisticated techniques such as carbon 14 dating, which can reveal how much time has passed since a plant or animal was alive. The approximate dates of archaeological sites also can be estimated through an examination of the sequence and context in which artifacts are found. If an archaeologist excavates a site to a depth of six feet, the artifacts he finds at the bottom of this pit would be older than those found near the surface. For this reason, the sequence, or order, in which an archaeologist recovers objects is very important. If an archaeologist discovers some points, knives, and scrapers at the bottom of a pit, stone tools as well as pottery at a depth of three feet, and metal tools near the surface, he might infer that the earliest people who lived there did not know how to make pottery or use metal, that they later developed the ability to make pottery (or another people who knew how moved onto the site), and that the most recent occupants used metal tools.

The archaeologist likewise takes into account all the evidence found at a particular level of an excavation in order to develop as complete a picture as possible of the people who lived at a site. If, in addition to pottery, he also finds corn kernels and cobs, stone hoes, hearths, and postholes set in a circular pattern, he might infer that the people who developed the pottery were farmers who built fairly permanent circular houses. If the site has been disturbed, that is, if someone interested solely in Indian pottery engaged in digging there and removed all the pieces of pottery, the archaeologist who scientifically excavates it will miss a significant achievement of the people who lived there and an important aspect of their life. Consequently, it is extremely important to report suspected archaeological sites so they can be investigated by trained professionals. Looting a site of its artifacts means that knowledge about the people who lived there hundreds and even thousands of years ago may be lost forever.

By excavating thousands of sites and examining millions of artifacts, archaeologists have discovered the way Native Americans lived during a particular time period and have been able to plot changes in their cultures.

This archaeologist is engaged in a 1948 excavation project at the Doerschuk site in the southern Piedmont of North Carolina. Photograph from Mark A. Mathis and Jeffrey J. Crow, eds., *The Prehistory of North Carolina: An Archaeological Symposium* (Raleigh: North Carolina Division of Archives and History, Department of Cultural Resources), fig. 2.4.

This excavation of a Mississippian platform mound was conducted by a team of archaeologists in western North Carolina. Photograph courtesy Research Laboratories of Anthropology, University of North Carolina at Chapel Hill.

Too often American Indians are thought of as frozen in time, but the natives whom Columbus encountered lived very differently from the hunters who crossed the Bering Strait Land Bridge during the Ice Age. In order to generalize about Native Americans and the changes they experienced, archaeologists distinguish certain cultural traditions, that is, periods of time in which large numbers of Indians shared certain characteristics. Scholars use the same technique to describe the past of other peoples. Historians, for example, refer to the period in Europe between the fall of Rome and the emergence of modern nation states (ca. A.D. 500–1500) as the Middle Ages. Because medieval practices endured longer in some parts of Europe than in others, dates are approximate. Similarly, cultural traditions endured longer in some parts of the Americas than in others or were present in some regions and not in others.

The first cultural tradition in North America, known as Paleo-Indian, lasted until about 8000 B.C. Although they probably gathered some wild foods and hunted smaller animals, Paleo-Indians were also

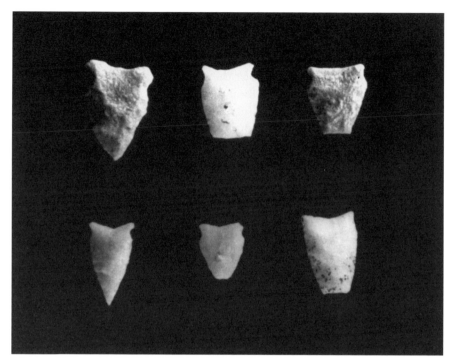

These projectile points, unearthed in an archaeological excavation, are typical of the late Paleo-Indian period in the Coastal Plain of North Carolina. Photograph from Mathis and Crow, *The Prehistory of North Carolina*, fig. 1.3.

big-game hunters. They followed herds of animals such as mammoths, camels, horses, and bison and killed their prey any way they could. The most effective method of killing large animals was by throwing or thrusting a spear at them at very close range. Paleo-Indians made points for their spears by flaking, or chipping, stone into the desired shape. In order to attach a point to a split shaft, they flattened, or fluted, it on each side. They used flaked stone knives and scrapers to cut up meat for food and prepare skins for clothing. Partly because they constantly had to follow animal herds, Paleo-Indians developed few other tools or utensils. They could not build and furnish permanent houses. They camped near the herds, and when the animals moved, so did they. A herd could support only a few people, so Paleo-Indians traveled and hunted in small bands. As a band became too large, it divided.

When Paleo-Indians came to North America, they traveled down the eastern slope of the Rocky Mountains and fanned out to populate the continent. There is some evidence that Paleo-Indians dwelt in North Carolina, particularly in the Piedmont but also in the Mountains and, although perhaps less so, in the Coastal Plain. These people left flaked points or axes or an occasional grinding stone, which was used to crush seeds and nuts, at the scattered sites they occupied. Such sites were often located on top of hills and ridges from which the Paleo-Indians depended primarily on animals for their livelihood and generally had to adapt their lives to the habits of their prey. They knew the value of plants and small animals for food, but they were not restricted to these resources because of the availability of large game.

About 8000 B.C. the Paleo-Indian tradition began to disappear in North America. The people, of course, did not disappear, but their way of life did because they no longer could hunt large game. A major climatic change occurred, and the Ice Age ended. A warming trend converted forest land into treeless plains or even deserts. In North Carolina the number of nut-producing and other deciduous trees increased as conifers (evergreen, cone-bearing trees) died out. The changes destroyed the habitats of many animals. Some, such as the mammoth and particular species of bison, became extinct; others, such as the camel and horse, ceased to exist in North America but continued to live elsewhere. Paleo-Indians, therefore, had far fewer large animals on which to subsist.

This problem was compounded by the population increase that Paleo-Indians experienced during the thousands of years they lived in North America. Two circumstances likely contributed to this population increase. First, the Americas had not been inhabited by humans before, and there was an abundance of game. People ate better and possibly lived longer, healthier lives than they had in Asia. Furthermore, those people who migrated to the Americas passed through very cold climates. Extremely low temperatures may have killed many disease-causing organisms, so that when people arrived in North America they were not as vulnerable to the many illnesses that had claimed lives in the Old World. As a result, mortality rates dropped. The human population grew and placed a greater demand on the animal population.

When many large game animals disappeared, Native Americans turned to smaller animals, shellfish, and wild plants for subsistence. Other changes accompanying the shift are significant enough to distinguish this new culture from that of Paleo-Indians. Archaeologists call the more recent cultural tradition Archaic. Archaic peoples were far more confined to particular regions than Paleo-Indians had been. In order to survive, Archaic peoples had to become intimately acquainted with their environment. They had to know which plants were edible and which were poisonous. They also had to observe and learn the habits of the small animals they killed. Archaic peoples in North Carolina, for example, would have known that the whitetail deer spends much of the day in the deep forest, emerging in late afternoon to feed in grassy clearings. If an Indian from the Great Plains, where there are no whitetail deer and no forests, had suddenly appeared, he might waste many valuable hours searching for game.

Even though Archaic peoples did not wander widely, they did move occasionally within the environment they knew. In spring they might camp near streams, where wild greens and onions sprouted. They might dwell near berry patches or fruit trees in summer and enter nut-bearing hardwood forests in fall. Because they moved so frequently, Archaic peoples did not build permanent houses or accumulate many possessions. They did, however, make extensive use of grinding stones and mortars to crush their nuts and seed.

Like Paleo-Indians, Archaic peoples in North Carolina did not make pottery. They did, however, carve bowls from soapstone. They probably did some cooking in pits lined with animal skins and filled with

Archaic peoples in North Carolina carved soapstone bowls such as the one pictured above. This example is over a foot in diameter. Photograph courtesy Office of State Archaeology, Raleigh, N.C.

water, into which they dropped heated stones. Many burned and cracked boiling stones have been found at Archaic sites in North Carolina. Archaic peoples also developed a new way to kill larger animals such as deer. They constructed an atlatl, or spear thrower, which, by artificially lengthening the arm, enabled them to hurl a spear with more force. To increase the force still more, Archaic man attached

Archaic peoples constructed atlatls, or spear throwers, which enabled them to hurl a spear with increased force. Use of the atlatl is shown in the drawing above. Archaic hunters also attached polished stone weights to atlatls, which increased still further the velocity of the hurled spear. Four of these stone weights are shown below. Drawing above by R. L. Hill, reproduced courtesy *South Carolina Wildlife*, Columbia, S.C.; photograph below courtesy Frank H. McClung Museum, University of Tennessee, Knoxville.

stone weights to the atlatl. Many of these weights have been found in North Carolina. The shape varies considerably, but all atlatl weights, or bannerstones, represent a technological advancement. Instead of merely chipping stones into rough forms, as Paleo-Indians did, Archaic peoples polished them with sand or other abrasives until they were smooth and shiny. They also polished their grinding stones and soapstone bowls. Archaic peoples added a number of other tools as well. They made polished axes with grooves, to which they attached handles. Archaic peoples demonstrated remarkable adaptation to their environment, but they nevertheless possessed little ability to control or modify that environment.

About 1000 B.C. there occurred in the Southeast an important development that enabled man to limit his migrations and establish more permanent homes. Agriculture appeared and dramatically changed the way man lived. For the first time, native peoples in the region began to demonstrate a decided preference for living near streams, where the rich alluvial soil could be farmed easily. This cultural tradition is known as the Woodland, and by 500 B.C. many of the people who lived in North Carolina had become part of it. These Woodland people cleared fields and planted squash, sunflowers, corn, pumpkins, and other vegetables. (Some Woodland people grew beans, but beans were not a major crop until about A.D. 1000.) Because they no longer had to migrate in search of food, Woodland people built permanent homes. Many constructed their houses by weaving saplings together into a framework and covering it with bark and skins. In the center of the houses, they dug fire pits and lined them with rocks.

Woodland people also began to make pottery, which they tempered, or strengthened, by adding crushed stone or sand to the clay. Woodland potters did not use a potter's wheel. Instead, they made long ropes of clay, which they coiled into the desired shape, smoothed with a stone, and then decorated. The type of decoration varied according to time and place. Some early Woodland people in Piedmont North Carolina wrapped a paddle with heavy fabric and pressed a design into wet clay pots; others wrapped a paddle with cord; and people of the later Woodland period cut, or incised, parallel lines into the clay with a sharp implement. Much Woodland pottery was in the shape of a round bowl or a jar with a pointed base.

In North Carolina, Woodland people continued to use atlatls for a time, but they gradually abandoned spears for a new device—the bow and arrow. The arrow required a much smaller and differently shaped

These examples of decorated tempered ceramics, made by Woodland people, were discovered primarily in the northern Coastal Plain of North Carolina. The ceramic sherd marked *a* and *f* are cord-marked; samples *b* and *d* are net-impressed; *c* is single-stamped; *e* is fabric-impressed; and *g* is incised. Photograph from Mathis and Crow, *The Prehistory of North Carolina*, fig. 1.6.

point than the spear. The earliest evidence of these new points in North Carolina has been found along the Yadkin River in the Piedmont.

One of the major characteristics associated with Woodland people in the eastern United States was their concern for the dead. In some areas they constructed burial mounds, earthen enclosures, or effigy mounds (mounds in the shape of animals) to honor the dead. Most Woodland people placed a variety of grave goods in their burial sites. In Piedmont

North Carolina, for example, Woodland people buried their dead in round or oval pits. They tied the body in a flexed position, that is, with the knees drawn tightly into the chest, and interred it with items such as shell necklaces or stone pipes.

The Woodland tradition was still alive in most of North Carolina when Europeans arrived. Most Woodland people lived in small villages along rivers. They grew a variety of crops, which they supplemented with fish, shellfish, and a variety of wild plants and game. They made pottery and built rather substantial houses. One aspect of their ritual life concerned honoring the dead. Priests, as illustrated by John White, spent much time and effort caring for the corpses of chiefs.

The other cultural tradition that existed in North Carolina at the time of European exploration and colonization made agriculture the focal point of religion. This tradition, known as the Mississippian, appeared about A.D. 700 along the Mississippi River and its tributaries. Mississippian people were far more dependent on farming than Woodland people, and their ceremonies centered on agricultural cycles. They commemorated the preparation of fields, planting, and harvest with religious rites.

Mississippian people held important rituals in ceremonial centers, where they constructed large pyramid-shaped mounds. Atop these mounds they built temples, and at the base they cleared public grounds for rituals, dancing, and ball games. Surrounding the ceremonial centers were houses and vegetable gardens, and beyond them lay large fields. When Europeans arrived, the Cherokees were a part of the Mississippian tradition, and even at the present time temple mounds can be seen in many river valleys of western North Carolina. Because there is little evidence of an invasion by Mississippian people in western North Carolina, the Indians who built these mounds probably were Woodland people who simply adopted the new tradition over a period of several hundred years.

In Piedmont North Carolina, however, an invasion by Mississippian people does appear to have occurred. That these people invaded, defeated, and drove Woodland Indians from their homes along the Pee Dee River is perhaps best explained by the more complex political organization prevalent in the Mississippian tradition. Possibly because of the manpower needed to build and maintain the ceremonial centers, Mississippian people developed large political units called chiefdoms. These chiefdoms united villages under far more powerful leadership than had existed among Woodland people, and they brought greater military might to bear on opponents. About the middle of the sixteenth

Town Creek Indian Mound, near Mt. Gilead in southern Montgomery County, North Carolina, was constructed by Mississippian people. It is presently open to the public as a state historic site operated by the North Carolina Office of Archives and History, Division of State Historic Sites and Properties. Photograph from the Town Creek Indian Mound, Mt. Gilead, N.C.

century (shortly before Sir Walter Raleigh attempted to establish a colony on Roanoke Island), a group of Mississippian people moved into the upper Pee Dee River valley. These people may have been ancestors of the Creek Indians, who in historic times lived in central Georgia and Alabama. They forced the indigenous Woodland (Siouan) people to take refuge in the hills and built large palisaded villages to protect themselves and their temple. One of the mounds built by the Mississippian people can be seen at the present time at Town Creek Indian Mound near Mt. Gilead. After an occupation of about a hundred years, however, they abandoned their fields and villages and returned to the south. The Woodland people, who were probably ancestral to the Siouan tribes of the historic period, subsequently reclaimed their land.

The link between prehistoric peoples and historic tribes is often difficult to determine, in part because the most recent period of prehistoric occupation is the one most likely to have been disturbed by subsequent development. In addition, observations by early writers were often inaccurate. With archaeologists and historians working together, however, the links gradually are being made. One thing is certain: the prehistoric occupants of North Carolina were the ancestors of historic Indians. Indians, not mound-building Celts or Scythians, crossed the Bering Strait, developed the atlatl and pottery, learned to use the bow and arrow, grew a variety of crops, and built great earthen mounds. Indians also guided early explorers, assisted European colonists, and attempted desperately to hold on to the land they had inhabited for thousands of years.

Chapter 2

THE INDIAN WAY OF LIFE

When Europeans first arrived in North Carolina, they encountered Woodland and Mississippian Indians who spoke several very different languages and belonged to many distinct tribes and villages. The languages of native Carolinians can be grouped into three families: Algonquian, Siouan, and Iroquoian. The speakers of Algonquian languages lived primarily along the coast, north of the Cape Fear River; Siouan-speaking tribes occupied the Cape Fear region and the Piedmont; and those who spoke Iroquoian lived between the Siouan and Algonquian tribes on the Coastal Plain and in the western mountains. Within these broad families were many different languages spoken by people who could not necessarily understand one another. Those who spoke only the Iroquoian language, Cherokee, could not understand the Iroquoian Tuscaroras. Moreover, specific languages often had several dialects. The Cherokees, for example, spoke at least three different dialects. Similarly, a common language did not necessarily produce political unity, as demonstrated in the early eighteenth century by the Tuscaroras, whose towns divided over the issue of war with the colonists. Many of the Carolina Indian tribes probably could communicate with each other by using interpreters or a simplified common language such as Mobilian, primarily a collection of Choctaw words used widely by southeastern Indians to conduct trade. The language barrier was not, therefore, insurmountable to Indians and did not inhibit trade and political alliances across linguistic boundaries.

Despite their linguistic diversity, native Carolinians shared certain cultural traits that often set them apart from Europeans. Indians, for example, wore few clothes; and their immodesty shocked many whites, who insisted on donning wool coats and half-suits of armor even on hot summer days. In their writings, Europeans carefully pointed out the Indians' presumed shortcomings, which ranged from improper table manners to immorality. At the present time, these Europeans are recognized as having been ethnocentric; that is, they were terribly biased in favor of their own way of doing things. Nevertheless, these ethnocentric Europeans must be relied upon for a great deal of information about native peoples because they provided the first written

These watercolors by John White depict an Indian elder or chief (*left*) and an Indian in body paint (*right*). From *The Drawings of John White, 1577–1590*, edited by Paul Hulton and David Beers Quinn. Published by the University of North Carolina Press, 1964. Copyright 1964 the Trustees of the British Museum. Used with permission of the publisher.

observations of American Indians. Even these flawed accounts provide far more information than the artifacts that are studied for earlier periods. But historians who examine these written sources must always remember that the authors often made mistakes in their interpretations of what they saw and experienced.

One of the first observations made by most white men concerned the Indians' color. John Lawson, who explored the North Carolina coast and Piedmont in the early eighteenth century, wrote: "Their Colour is of a tawny, which would not be so dark, did they not daub themselves with Bears Oil, and a Colour like burnt cork . . . which fills the Pores." The trader James Adair expanded Lawson's explanation: "The Parching winds and hot sun-beams heating upon their naked bodies, in their various gradations of life, necessarily tarnish their skins with the tawny red color." The comments of Lawson and Adair may seem silly at the present time, but it must be remembered that they knew nothing about skin pigmentation or genetics. On the other hand, native Carolinians employed a variety of practices to transform their physical appearance, which early observers sometimes believed the Indians had inherited. Because no razors existed, men plucked their facial hair with clamshell tweezers, a practice that led Europeans to believe that Indian men had no beards. Similarly, some Indian women bound children to cradle boards and by wrapping or placing weights on the children's foreheads, deformed their skulls without impairing intelligence so that children would conform to the Indians' notion of ideal beauty. This latter practice may seem cruel, but it should also be noted that many modern children endure years of metal-filled mouths so that they can have abnormally straight teeth. Early European observers, however, could not separate cultural practices from genetic traits or vice versa. Modern science has provided important insights into racial differences and similarities. Furthermore, anthropology, the study of man, has helped to shape an understanding of differences among human cultures.

Culture is the learned behavior of a society; that is, culture consists of those things such as religion or language that are not inherited biologically (for example, skin color). Culture is transmitted from one generation to the next by example and education. Whites soon discovered that many Indian practices that they believed stemmed from biology actually were cultural.

Europeans who came to North Carolina were part of a culture characterized by Christianity, constitutional monarchy, a commercial economy, patriarchal (or male-dominated) households, and considerable freedom for and emphasis upon the individual. The native Carolina cultures that these Europeans encountered were quite different. The Indians had little notion of monotheism, or belief in one god. Led rather than ruled, they governed themselves through open councils that arrived at decisions by consensus. Their religious and ethical systems condemned acquisitiveness and reinforced a subsistence-level economy in which people produced only enough for survival. Women had considerable power and influence within the family and, among some native peoples, within the tribe as a whole. Finally, while Carolina Indians had considerable personal freedom, the well-being of the community normally took precedence over the desires of any individual.

Native Carolinians did not separate religion from the other aspects of their lives. They believed that a variety of spirits, some more powerful than others, inhabited the world and that these spirits had to be placated. Consequently, many of their everyday activities took on religious significance. A Cherokee warrior always asked forgiveness from the deer he killed so that the deer's spirit would not bring disease to him or his family. Similarly the Siouan people ceremonially burned the bones from meat so that the game would remain in their locale.

Most human burial customs also were intended to appease the spirits of the dead. Just as people and game had spirits, so did the sun, crops, and even thunder. It was man's responsibility to invoke the aid of these spirits and avoid their vengeful wrath.

Man had the ability to tap supernatural power for his own use, but such an act required him to be spiritually pure. Because Indians associated spiritual purity and physical cleanliness, bathing was at least partly a religious act. Failure to maintain spiritual purity or contact with polluting substances (such as blood) could bring on adversity. Therefore, a person who was suspected of impurity, such as a warrior, often spent days bathing, fasting, and purging himself in order to cleanse his spirit. Indians believed pollution could be sent by others through conjuring, which could result in illness and death. Ridding a person of such a spell often involved spending time in a sweathouse or drinking a variety of decoctions.

Ceremonies were usually designed to purify an entire group as well as honor some particular spirit. The major event in the religious life of many native Carolinians was the Green Corn Ceremony. Held in the late summer when the corn could first be eaten, this ceremony commemorated the new crop. It was also an occasion for people to clean the council house and their family homes, thereby symbolically cleansing their environment. They fasted and then bathed, extinguished old fires and rekindled new ones, and forgave most wrongs done them in the preceding year. Carolina Indians entered their new year with themselves spiritually cleansed and their social relationships repaired.

An important aspect of the Green Corn Ceremony was the destruction of any food left over from the preceding year. By throwing this food out, Indians prevented the accumulation of a surplus. Similarly they hunted not to stockpile meat and skins, but out of necessity. Furthermore, personal belongings often were buried with the dead rather than inherited by descendants. These acts, plus a general suspicion of anyone who was too successful (he might be using supernatural powers), compelled native Carolinians to live simply and modestly. There were few distinctions based on wealth; and because surpluses benefited no one, the Indians gladly gave food to anyone in need, including European explorers and colonists.

The Indians made their living by hunting, fishing, farming, and gathering. The major game animal was the deer. At the time Europeans arrived, very large herds of deer, sometimes numbering in the hundreds,

White's "Theire sitting at meate" depicts an Indian man and woman eating. From *The Drawings of John White, 1577–1590*, edited by Paul Hulton and David Beers Quinn. Published by the University of North Carolina Press, 1964. Copyright 1964 the Trustees of the British Museum. Used with permission of the publisher.

roamed the Southeast. In many areas, native Carolinians carefully burned the underbrush in the forests to flush out the hunted deer and, in turn, encourage the growth of tender grass on which these herds grazed. While deer normally could be found near villages, many Indian men also participated in long winter hunts, during which they traveled hundreds of miles over several months. They killed the deer with bows and arrows and brought home dried meat, skins, and bones for a variety of uses. They roasted meat over open fires or cooked it in stews. The deerskins provided clothing and blankets, and the bones and antlers became tools—hoe blades, arrow points, awls, or needles. The Indians even used deer sinew as thread and hooves for glue. They tried to waste nothing.

In addition to deer, native Carolinians also killed wild turkeys, which provided not only food but also feathers for ceremonial wands and cloaks, which were made by tying feathers to fiber netting. They also hunted bear, usually by trapping instead of shooting them. The Indians ate the meat, cured the bearskins, made the claws into ornaments, and rendered the fat for use as a substitute for butter. Carolina Indians also killed smaller animals such as rabbits, squirrels, or birds. Sometimes they trapped these animals, and other times, notably among the Cherokees, they killed them with blowguns—long hollow reeds through which they blew darts.

*A cheife Heroroans wyfe of Pomeoc.
and her daughter of the age of .8. or.
.10 . yeares .*

White's drawing of an Indian woman and young girl shows the woman clutching a gourd and the girl holding a doll. From *The Drawings of John White, 1577–1590*, edited by Paul Hulton and David Beers Quinn. Published by the University of North Carolina Press, 1964. Copyright 1964 the Trustees of the British Museum. Used with permission of the publisher.

Fishing supplemented their diet, particularly in the summer. While hunting was done exclusively by men, women often joined the men in fishing. They used hooks, nets, and traps to catch fish. Sometimes the Indians constructed a barricade across a stream and then chased the fish downstream into the waiting pool. There they speared them or used a poison that paralyzed them but did not make them inedible. At other times, particularly along the coast, Indians fished at night from dugout canoes in which they had built a small fire on wet sand. The firelight attracted fish, and the fishermen speared them. There are even accounts of Indians lassoing sturgeons, very large fish that once were plentiful in the tidewater, and then riding them until they tired and could be heaved ashore.

Men and women also worked together in the fields, although among the Cherokees and some other tribes women performed most of the agricultural labor. Their tools were stone hoes or pointed sticks, and their crops included corn, beans, squash, pumpkins, and sunflowers. Corn was the most important crop and was the staple in the Indian diet. While some corn was eaten green, most was allowed to ripen or dry in the fields before it was harvested. The women then soaked the hard kernels in lye (made by dripping water through wood ashes) to remove the husks and cause them to swell. Then they rinsed the corn, dried it, and pounded it into meal. The meal became the basis for bread, to which dried beans and nuts were added, and for soups or stews. Women also did most of the gathering of wild food. They picked fresh tender greens and wild onions in spring and berries and fruit in summer. In fall they gathered nuts and, along with the men, searched for honey trees. Throughout the year women gathered firewood and carried water.

The women did not seem to mind working in the fields and doing the many other chores for which they were responsible. In spite of the heavy work, they may have seen themselves as occupying a special position because the kinship system of native Carolinians was matrilineal, that is, traced through women rather than men (or, as is done at present, through both men and women). A child's relatives were those to whom he was directly linked by his mother—his brothers and sisters, his mother's brothers and sisters, and his mother's mother. He was not considered to be related by blood to his father or his father's family. As a result, women probably had a major if not dominant role in the operation of the household. Furthermore, the frequent absences of men who were hunting, on the warpath, or at the council house, meant that domestic matters were left largely to women.

The houses over which women presided were usually made of bark or a kind of clapboard with bark or thatch roofs. The Cherokees, who lived in a colder climate, also constructed winter houses—small, windowless earthen lodges that they warmed with a small fire. Other Indians built similar structures, but they were used as sweat lodges for medical and religious purposes rather than as shelter from the winter cold. Native Carolinians usually furnished their houses with woven straw or cane mats, benches, clay pottery, baskets, and various wooden utensils.

The towne of Pomeiock and true forme of their howses, couered and enclosed some wth matts, and some wth barcks of trees. All compassed abowt wth smale poles stock thick together in stedd of a wall.

The Indian village of Pomeiock, according to this drawing by John White, consisted of a number of houses surrounded by a circular protective palisade of poles partially buried in the ground. From *The Drawings of John White, 1577–1590*, edited by Paul Hulton and David Beers Quinn. Published by the University of North Carolina Press, 1964. Copyright 1964 the Trustees of the British Museum. Used with permission of the publisher.

The Indians erected their houses and villages close to rivers or streams where water, fish, and fertile land were most abundant. Some Indians grouped their houses close together and surrounded them with a protective palisade, while others scattered their homesites for a mile or more alongside a river. Whether villages were compact or extended, certain public buildings provided a focal point for their inhabitants. Villages normally supported council houses, in which public meetings took place. The Cherokees built their council houses of wood and clay along the lines of their winter houses, while the Waxhaws built thatched council houses with pyramidal roofs. Among many tribes, council houses were merely larger versions of dwellings.

The Waxhaws invited John Lawson to their council house for a ceremony that involved dancing and feasting. The interior was very dark, since the only light came from a small fire in the central hearth. Each household brought food for the banquet, and all Indians in the village seem to have participated in the festivities. The men, accompanied by a drum made of an earthen pot covered with taut deerskin, performed an hour-long dance in which they wore masks and pretended to engage in combat. Then a musician with a gourd rattle joined the drummer in providing music for the women, who wore bells around their ankles and necks. They danced for six hours while the musicians recounted the history of the tribe.

Lawson, who visited many other coastal tribes, reported that "in these State-Houses is transacted all Publick and Private Business, relating to the Affairs of the Government, as the Audience of Foreign Ambassadors from other Indian Rulers, Consultation of waging and making War, Proposals of their Trade with neighbouring Indians, or the English, who happened to come amongst them." John Lederer, who explored the interior of North Carolina in the late seventeenth century, noted that the forms of government that existed among Carolina tribes varied widely. The Occaneechis, he found, had two chiefs, "one presiding in arms, the other in hunting and husbandry." He reported that the Waterees, a tribe later incorporated into the Catawbas, differed "in government from all the other Indians of these parts: for they are slaves, rather than subjects to their king." The Eno tribe, on the other hand, enjoyed a democratic government.

In most tribal governments, the village council played a prominent role. Villagers met in the council house and discussed issues at length. They did not choose a course of action, according to Lawson, "without a great deal of Deliberation and Wariness." Anyone who wished to

Their rype corne

Their greene corne

Corne newly sprong

Their sitting at meate

The place of solemne prayer

The house wherin the Tombe of their Herounds standeth

SECOTON

A Ceremony in their prayers wth strange testiers and songs danfing abowt posts carued on the topps lyke mens faces.

White's depiction of the Indian village of Secoton shows the systematic manner in which the Indians used different portions of their village for various specific purposes. From *The Drawings of John White, 1577–1590*, edited by Paul Hulton and David Beers Quinn. Published by the University of North Carolina Press, 1964. Copyright 1964 the Trustees of the British Museum. Used with permission of the publisher.

White's "Indians Dancing" shows how Native Americans used spears and gourd-filled rattles as part of their dance ceremony. From *The Drawings of John White, 1577–1590*, edited by Paul Hulton and David Beers Quinn. Published by the University of North Carolina Press, 1964. Copyright 1964 the Trustees of the British Museum. Used with permission of the publisher.

speak did so, and no one interrupted him. Prominent warriors or elderly people who were respected for their knowledge and wisdom could influence the course of a debate through the esteem the villagers had for them, but they rarely could force people to follow them. A consensus usually emerged from the discussion.

The most serious topic discussed by councils was war. Indians went to war to avenge the deaths of kinsmen who had been killed by an enemy. Believing that the spirits of the dead could not rest until those responsible had died, native Carolinians viewed war not only as an act of patriotism but also as a religious obligation. The size of war parties ranged from two or three men to as many as one hundred. Their object was to surprise the enemy and take their revenge without losing any of their own warriors. While on the warpath, they imitated the movements of animals and communicated by means of birdcalls to avoid detection by the enemy. When they finally attacked, the warriors tried to kill or injure as many of the enemy as they had lost among their own people.

White's drawing of an Indian charnel house is accompanied by his written explanation of the manner in which the Indians prepared the bodies of their dead. From *The Drawings of John White, 1577–1590*, edited by Paul Hulton and David Beers Quinn. Published by the University of North Carolina Press, 1964. Copyright 1964 the Trustees of the British Museum. Used with permission of the publisher.

In the late sixteenth century, Thomas Harriot gave the following description of Indian warfare:

Their manner of wars among themselves is either by suddenly surprising one another most commonly about the dawning of the day, or moonlight, or else by ambushes, or some subtle devices. Set battles are very rare, except it fall out that where there are many trees, where either part may have some hope of defense, after the delivery of every arrow, in leaping behind some or other.

Indians often scalped and dismembered victims so that they could offer proof to villagers and the spirits of the dead that they had done their duty. Sometimes warriors took prisoners back to a village, where the entire community had an opportunity to participate in the revenge by torturing the unfortunate captive to death. In 1711, during a war between the Tuscaroras and the Carolina colonists, John Lawson was captured and tortured to death.

Despite the cruelty of torture, Indian warfare was no more horrible than its European counterpart and may well have been shorter in duration and involved fewer participants. For Indians, war was merely a raid. These raids back and forth among tribes and villages went on continually, but rarely before European contact were entire populations mobilized and entire countries laid waste.

The arrival of Europeans dramatically changed the Indian way of life. Confronted with a far more aggressive culture that possessed certain technological advantages, the Indians struggled at first to accommodate the intruders and then to expel them. In the end, neither tactic proved very successful.

Chapter 3

INDIAN-WHITE RELATIONS

Native Carolinians came into contact with Europeans less than fifty years after Columbus entered the New World. At first the object of curiosity, Indians soon became suppliers of food and furs to the newcomers and customers for a wide variety of European manufactured goods. While the impact of trade on native cultures and societies was significant, more devastating changes occurred as the result of European warfare and disease, which decimated the Indian population of North Carolina.

Experts have estimated, based on archaeological evidence, that between 50,000 and 100,000 Native Americans lived within the present-day borders of North Carolina at the moment of contact. The actual number may be much higher. As Giovanni da Verrazano sailed along the Carolina coast in 1524 under the French flag, he "saw everywhere very great fires, by reason of the multitude of the inhabitants." Sixty years later, Ralph Lane, exploring Carolina for Sir Walter Raleigh, who hoped to plant a colony there, wrote that "the continent is of a huge and unknown greatness and very well peopled and towned." Although the native population at the time of these explorations is unknown, it is believed that the number of Indians soon declined rapidly. Historical demographers, people who study past populations, have theorized that for every one hundred Indians at the time of European contact, only five existed two hundred years later.

One major cause of depopulation was disease. Native peoples had had no contact with the deadly pestilences of Europe; therefore, they had developed no immunities to smallpox, bubonic plague, typhus, or even less serious ailments such as measles. Consequently, they contracted these diseases far more readily than Europeans, and their chances for survival were far less. Smallpox in particular took a terrible toll. In 1695 an epidemic virtually wiped out the Pamlico Indians, and in 1738 smallpox killed half the Cherokees. The Cherokees undoubtedly increased the mortality rate through their treatment of this strange new disease: medicine men alternated between placing patients in sweat-houses and plunging them into cold rivers. Even measles, a relatively mild disease among Europeans, who had some immunity to it, killed thousands of Native Americans.

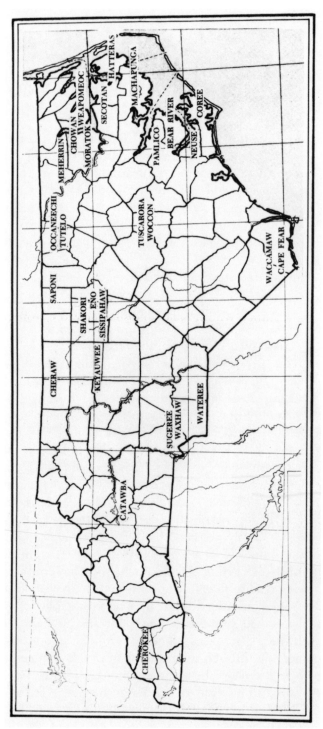

This map shows the approximate locations of various Indian groups in North Carolina, 1600–1700, the period of initial European contact. From Ruth Y. Wetmore, *First on the Land: The North Carolina Indians* (Winston-Salem: John F. Blair, 1975), fig. 2; reproduced courtesy John F. Blair.

Another factor in the depopulation of Carolina was warfare. Indians, of course, had fought among themselves, but the intensity of warfare increased dramatically with the arrival of Europeans. Europeans, who considered themselves to be vastly superior to native Carolinians, therefore took little time to try to understand the Indians' culture. Instead, when Indians behaved in a way that Europeans thought was inappropriate, the white men ruthlessly punished them. In 1585, during the second expedition sent by Sir Walter Raleigh to Carolina, an Indian "stole" a silver cup from the Englishmen. Actually, the Indian may have believed the cup was a gift or community property. In any event, the English retaliated against the Indian's village. According to the English leader, Ralph Lane, "we burned and spoiled their corn and town, all the people fled." While there were no immediate Indian casualties in this attack, many villagers may have died from the hunger and exposure that followed the destruction of their homes and crops.

Trade with the Indians also gave rise to warfare. Commercial relations between native Carolinians and Europeans began very early. The first group of Englishmen whom Raleigh dispatched to Carolina in

European manufactured artifacts such as these were traded to Indians, who increasingly came to depend upon such goods. The items pictured here include (*left*) a rum or wine bottle; (*upper right*) a hoe and tomahawk; and (*lower right*) a bone-handled fork, a Jew's harp, and brass tinklers. Photograph by Institute of Archaeology and Anthropology, University of South Carolina, Columbia; reproduced in Charles Hudson, *The Southeastern Indians* (Knoxville: University of Tennessee Press, 1976), fig. 104.

1584 discovered that a handsome profit could be made in the Indian trade. Arthur Barlowe, captain of one of the ships sent on the expedition, reported to Raleigh: "We exchanged our tin dish for twenty skins, worth twenty crowns or twenty nobles, and a copper kettle for fifty skins, worth fifty crowns. They offered us good exchange for our hatchets and axes and for knives, and would have given anything for swords, but we would not depart with any." These explorers were selling relatively inexpensive items for exorbitant prices. In the early eighteenth century John Lawson complained that in trade with the Indians, white traders "daily cheat them in everything we sell, and esteem it a Gift of Christianity not to sell them so cheap as we do to the Christians, as we call ourselves." Seventy years later the situation had not improved. James Adair, himself a trader, protested the colonial government's granting of "general licenses to mean reprobate peddlars by which they [the Indians] are inebriated, and cheated." This kind of behavior on the part of white traders did not win friends among the Indians and sometimes provoked them to violence.

However unscrupulous most traders were, the Indians came to depend on the goods that white men sold. Most native Carolinians considered metal hoes to be a vast improvement over simple digging sticks, and metal knives and hatchets obviously had advantages over similar stone tools. Guns and ammunition quickly replaced bows and arrows among tribes trading with Europeans, and any tribe that did not obtain these weapons was at the mercy of better-armed enemies.

Except for the coastal region, most North Carolina Indians conducted their business with traders from Virginia or South Carolina. In 1728 William Byrd, a prominent Virginia planter, gave the following account of commercial relations with Carolina Indians:

Gentlemen send for Goods proper for such a Trade from England, and then either Venture them out at their own Risk to the Indian Towns, or else credit some Traders with them of Substance and Reputation, to be paid in Skins at a certain Price agreed betwixt them.

The Goods for the Indian Trade consist chiefly in Guns, Powder, Shot, Hatchets (which the Indians call Tomahawks,) Kettles, red and blue Planes, Duffields, Stroudwater blankets, and some Cutlary Wares, Brass rings and other Trinkets.

Their Wares are made up into Packs and Carry'd upon Horses, each Load being from 150 to 200 Pounds, with which they are able to travel about 20 miles a day, if Forage happens to be plentiful.

Formerly a Hundred Horses have been employ'd in one of these Indian Caravans, under the conduct of 15 or 16 Persons only, but now the Trade is much impair'd, insomuch that they seldom go with half that Number. . . .

They commonly reside among the Indians till they have barter'd their Goods away for Skins, with which they load their Horses and come back the Same Path they went.

Although the Indians sold traders some corn and handicrafts such as baskets, the major item of exchange was deerskins. Europeans used deerskins to make a variety of leather goods, and the demand for skins seemed insatiable. The Indians began killing more and more deer. As a consequence of this intensive hunting, the number of deer began to decline, and Indians had to travel further from their villages in order to satisfy the demand for deerskins. They hunted anywhere deer might be found—even near white settlements. Because this increased the likelihood of hostilities, North Carolina colonists attempted to prevent Indians from hunting along the frontier. Laws that prohibited Indians from hunting near white settlements so distressed coastal tribes that in 1740 many Indians threatened to leave North Carolina, to the dismay of local traders.

Another problem arose from the deerskin trade. Because Indians hunted deer primarily in winter, when the skins were heaviest, traders often permitted them to make purchases year round and then collected for these purchases at the end of the winter hunt. Frequently, the skins from the hunt did not cover the debts accumulated during the previous year. Traders demanded payment, but the Indians could not pay. Once again, the likelihood of violence was great. For this reason, North Carolina tried (with little success) to prevent traders from extending credit to the Indians. In 1736 the colonial government appointed two commissioners to supervise the Indian trade and "ordered that for the future the Indian Traders do not presume to trust or give any credit to the Indians."

Next to deerskins, the most important commodity Indians traded to whites was war captives, whom Europeans used as slaves alongside Africans on their plantation. The desire to capture other Indians for sale to white traders led to a marked increase in warfare among various tribes. In 1714 two traders encouraged a group of Cherokees who were in debt to them to raid Chestowe, a village of the neighboring Yucchi Indians. After the traders deceived the warriors by claiming falsely that the governor of South Carolina had authorized the raid, the Cherokees attacked and captured enough slaves to pay their debts. The promise of slaves also encouraged many Yamasee warriors from South Carolina to join with whites against the North Carolina Tuscaroras in the Tuscarora War of 1711–1713. The increase in intertribal warfare and the sale of many

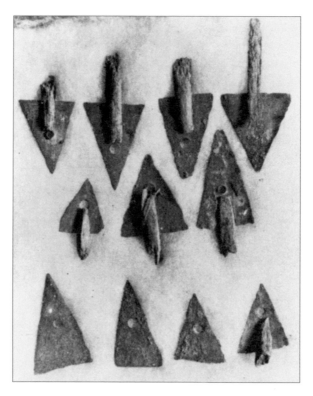

These brass arrowheads were cut from kettles traded to Indians during the eighteenth century. Photograph reproduced courtesy Frank H. McClung Museum.

Indians into slavery further reduced the number of free native Carolinians.

The Indians' dependence on trade meant that they could be manipulated by traders and colonial officials. The colonial governments often used the Indian trade to compel tribes to surrender runaway slaves or natives accused of crimes against whites. The threat to suspend trade usually was enough to convince a particular tribe to remain neutral or form an alliance with the English in intertribal or colonial wars. The upper Tuscaroras, who lived north of the Pamlico River, did not join the Tuscaroras south of the river in their war against the English in part because of the Indian trade. The northern Tuscaroras acted as middle-men in the profitable trade between Virginia merchants and tribes to the south and west. Not willing to jeopardize this lucrative position, these Tuscaroras remained neutral.

Although there had been a series of skirmishes, the Tuscarora War was the first major conflict between native Carolinians and white colonists. The Tuscaroras controlled much of the territory between the

Roanoke and Neuse rivers. Traditionally, their villages had been largely independent from one another, but the pressure of European settlements forced the villages into confederations that also included some of the small, displaced coastal tribes. The Tuscaroras between the Pamlico and Roanoke rivers banded together under the leadership of Chief Tom Blunt, while villages between the Pamlico and the Neuse followed Chief Hancock.

The southern Tuscaroras under Hancock felt greater pressure from white settlement than did the upper towns, particularly when whites began to settle at the mouth of the Neuse River in 1701. In 1710 a large group of Swiss and German colonists located near the southern Tuscaroras and built the town of New Bern. Because the government of the colony rested at that time in the hands of men intent upon pushing the frontier westward, political affairs in the colony contributed to Indian anxiety. The southern Tuscaroras began to fear for their tribal domain. Moreover, the escalation of the Indian slave trade in the early 1700s damaged Indian-white relations in the region. Consequently, Chief Hancock believed that the Indians' only recourse was war.

Chief Hancock planned his attack for September 1711. Before he moved against the colonists, however, he captured John Lawson; Baron Christoph von Graffenried, leader of the Swiss and German colonists; and an African American servant who had traveled from New Bern to explore the interior of Carolina. The Tuscaroras executed Lawson and held the other two captive, preventing them from sounding the alarm. On September 22, Hancock's warriors attacked white settlements in Bath County. They killed about 120 colonists, took others captive, seized crops and livestock, and burned houses and barns. Gov. Edward Hyde and his counselors, enjoying the relative safety of Albemarle County, did little to aid the colonists in Bath. Local whites retaliated, and finally in January 1712, South Carolina sent a company of Yamasees, other Indians, and whites under the command of Col. John Barnwell to subdue the southern Tuscaroras. Barnwell's forces captured Fort Narhantes, a Tuscarora stronghold, after a bitter battle. The invading soldiers failed to take Fort Hancock, but the Indians nevertheless agreed to a truce. During a subsequent conference, however, Barnwell's troops killed fifty Tuscarora men and seized about two hundred women and children as slaves. This act of treachery led to renewed hostilities, which raged throughout the summer. The desperate Carolina colonists promised Tom Blunt of the northern Tuscaroras control over the entire tribe in exchange for his collaboration. Blunt accepted the offer and captured Hancock, whom the colonists executed. In the spring of

This pen drawing with black wash (ca. 1711) shows Baron Christoph von Graffenried, John Lawson, and their African American servant held as captives by the Tuscarora Indians. From Franz Louis Michel, *Relations du voyage d'Amèrique que le Baron de Graffenried a fait en y amenant une colonie Palatine et Suisse, et son retour en Europe*; original held by Burgerbibliothek, Bern, Switzerland.

1713, Col. James Moore of South Carolina attacked Fort Neoheroka and killed or captured more than nine hundred Tuscaroras in the successful assault. The surviving southern Tuscaroras were forced onto a reservation near Lake Mattamuskeet in present-day Hyde County, but throughout the eighteenth century, groups of Tuscaroras moved north to join the Iroquois, a powerful confederacy of related tribes in New York and southern Canada.

Many of the Tuscaroras who remained in North Carolina had been neutral or even friendly to the colonists during the Tuscarora War, but white Carolinians quickly forgot the services that they had rendered. Confined to a reservation on the lower Roanoke River, the northern Tuscaroras saw their land base threatened and their people despised by neighboring whites. In 1752 Moravian bishop August Gottlieb Spangenberg reported that the Tuscaroras and other Indians of eastern Carolina were "in a bad way." The Chowan Indians, he wrote, "are reduced to a few families, and their land has been taken away." The Meherrins "are also reduced to a mere handful." The Tuscaroras had managed to hold on to "a pretty piece of land," but, the bishop noted, "they live in great poverty, and are oppressed by the whites." All the

Several Cherokee chiefs, including Attakullakulla (*far right*), visited London in 1730. This engraving by Isaac Basire, after a painting by Markham, records the visit. Engraving courtesy Smithsonian Institution, Washington, D.C.

Indians he visited looked "as if they were under a curse that crushes them."

Bishop Spangenberg expressed sympathy for the plight of these remnants of once powerful tribes, but he also seemed convinced that they were doomed to extinction. In order to profit from their demise, he proposed that the Moravians secure a grant to Tuscarora land from Lord Granville, the remaining proprietor of Carolina. He made clear that the Moravian Brethren would take possession of the land only after the Indians vacated it. If the normally humanitarian Moravians could look with such covetousness upon Tuscarora land, imagine how little respect frontier whites, who viewed Indians as savages, had for their property rights, particularly as land increasingly replaced deerskins and captives as the Indian possession most desired by whites. Unable to contend with the pressure exerted on them, the remaining Tuscaroras finally abandoned their land in North Carolina in 1803 and joined their kinsmen on reservations in New York and Canada.

The Tuscaroras had been the most powerful tribe between the Carolina coast and the Appalachian Mountains. Their defeat opened the interior of North Carolina to white settlement, and in the half century following the Tuscarora War, colonists pushed relentlessly westward.

The next serious Indian threat encountered by the whites came from the Cherokees, who lived in the mountain valleys of western North Carolina, up-country South Carolina, north Georgia, and east Tennessee.

While the English quickly dominated the coastal Carolina tribes, the Cherokees maintained their independence throughout the colonial period. They were able to do so in part because they had a large population and lived in a remote, defensible region. Furthermore, the Cherokees traded with the French colony of Louisiana and with the Spanish in Florida, which made them less dependent on English trade goods. For many years the Cherokees played one European power against the other with some success. Failure to make a formal alliance with one of these European countries, however, made the Cherokees fair game for warriors from tribes that had negotiated such alliances.

In the mid-eighteenth century the Cherokees suffered in particular from attacks by Choctaw and Shawnee allies of the French. As a result, leaders of a number of Cherokee towns asked the English to construct forts and station garrisons in their territory to protect their homes and families while warriors were away retaliating against the enemy. The English welcomed the opportunity to build these forts, which served not only to protect the Indians but also to prevent French infiltration and defend the backcountry. In 1756 they built Fort Prince George in South Carolina and Fort Loudoun in present-day east Tennessee. At about the same time, the colonial government of North Carolina constructed Fort Dobbs near present-day Statesville to offer protection to the frontier. It is now a state historic site.

Upon completion of the forts, the Cherokees agreed to send about one hundred warriors to join an expedition against the Shawnees, who lived along the Ohio River. After six weeks, heavy snows and swollen rivers forced the warriors to turn back. They had lost their horses and provisions while on the campaign, and to avoid starvation, they killed some cattle foraging in the forest along the Virginia frontier. The white frontiersmen who owned the livestock then attacked the Cherokees, killed several, and scalped them. Adding insult to injury, the frontiersmen claimed that the scalps belonged to enemy Indians and sold them to the Virginia government, which routinely paid for enemy scalps.

Enraged young Cherokee warriors began raiding frontier settlements and forts, including Fort Dobbs, to avenge the deaths of their tribesmen. Older headmen attempted to restrain them and sent a delegation to Charleston in 1758 to arrange a truce. Nevertheless, the raids continued. In November 1759, thirty-two of the most prominent men in the tribe met the governor of South Carolina at Fort Prince George to work out

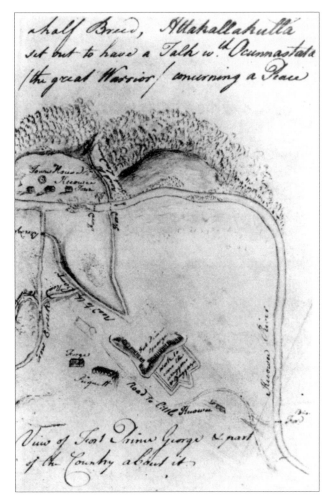

This map shows a "View of Fort Prince George & part of the Country about it." The South Carolina outpost was the site of a significant Indian-white confrontation in 1759. Illustration from Duane H. King and E. Raymond Evans, eds., "Memoirs of the Grant Expedition against the Cherokees in 1761," *Journal of Cherokee Studies*, 2 (Summer 1977), 281; reproduced courtesy Museum of the Cherokee Indian, Cherokee.

an acceptable agreement. The governor promptly imprisoned them in a room that customarily housed six soldiers and demanded the surrender of all belligerent Cherokees. A few concessions by the Cherokees led the governor to release three Indians, including the war chief Oconostota, who immediately organized a siege of the fort. When Cherokee warriors mounted an assault, the soldiers inside massacred the Indian hostages.

In retaliation, the Cherokees accelerated their attacks along the frontier and began a siege of Fort Loudoun. In June 1760, British colonel Archibald Montgomery, who had been sent from New York to aid the Carolina colonists, and 1,600 soldiers invaded Cherokee territory, destroyed all the towns in South Carolina, slaughtered more than a hundred Cherokees, and drove the survivors into the mountains. Montgomery then advanced toward the North Carolina towns. A few miles from present-day Franklin, a large force of Cherokee warriors ambushed the company, killed nearly one hundred Englishmen, and forced Montgomery to retreat to Fort Prince George.

The defeat of Montgomery's force doomed Fort Loudoun. Cut off from help and reduced to eating horses and dogs, members of the garrison surrendered in late summer. The soldiers agreed to turn over all guns and ammunition to the Indians in exchange for a promise of safe conduct to the English settlements. However, the soldiers buried most of their weapons inside the fort or threw them into the river. This duplicity sealed their fate. The next day, the Cherokees struck at dawn, killed thirty of the soldiers, and took the others captive.

The following summer (1761), Col. James Grant launched another expedition against the Cherokees. A force of 2,600 men, including Chickasaw and Catawba warriors, defeated the Cherokees. Grant ordered the destruction of the North Carolina Cherokee towns, and detachments burned houses and corncribs, shot or stole livestock, and laid waste the cornfields. Famine and epidemic followed this invasion. According to some estimates, war, hunger, and disease reduced the Cherokee population to one-half its prewar total. The Cherokees made peace in 1761, but their difficulties did not end. In a series of treaties and land sales, the Cherokees relinquished their vast hunting grounds in present-day Virginia, West Virginia, Kentucky, and middle Tennessee.

The Cherokee War was only one phase of a larger North American conflict known as the French and Indian War, which ended in 1763. In this war, the French and their Indian allies fought the British. The British had not been as successful as the French in recruiting native warriors because the Indians realized that the French were content with trade, while the British wanted their land. The British won the war, although it cost them dearly. Aware that colonial land hunger had caused many Indians to favor France, the British king in 1763 prohibited white settlement beyond the crest on the Appalachian Mountains. This royal proclamation infuriated the colonists, particularly those in North Carolina who wanted to move into east Tennessee, but it pleased the Cherokees. For this reason, most Cherokees sided with the British during the American Revolution, and once again Cherokee war parties raided the frontier.

In 1776 the colonists staged a four-pronged invasion of Cherokee territory. Although they encountered only scattered resistance, North Carolina soldiers under the command of Gen. Griffith Rutherford demolished more than fifty Cherokee towns. They killed and scalped women as well as men and sold children into slavery. The Cherokees who survived fled to the mountains, where they were exposed to the elements and subsisted on whatever wild food they could gather. Following this devastating campaign, the majority of Cherokees favored peace and agreed to relinquish all lands east of the Blue Ridge.

The American Revolution brought independence to white Carolinians, but by the end of the war native Carolinians were a conquered people. Economically dependent upon the British at first, Indian people ultimately succumbed to the invader's military might. The consequences were far-reaching for native Carolinians. The Tuscaroras migrated from the state, and smaller Indian groups along the coast existed merely on the periphery of white society—exploited when possible but largely ignored by surrounding whites. Historically, these small native communities remained almost invisible until the late nineteenth or early twentieth century, when they reasserted their ethnic identity. The Cherokees, however, managed to maintain a semblance of political independence and cultural integrity, even in the face of military defeat.

Chapter 4

THE CHEROKEE

By the end of the American Revolution, the Cherokees were in dire straits. Invading armies had razed many villages, destroyed stores of food, and drastically reduced the population. Furthermore, the tribe's cession of enormous tracts of land made infeasible an economy based on hunting and trading. The Cherokees, therefore, looked to the future with fear and uncertainty. What the future held for them was a cultural transformation. In less than half a century, many Cherokees abandoned their aboriginal way of life and constructed a new society modeled on that of the white South.

The Cherokees embarked on this course during the administration of George Washington. Washington and his advisers adopted a policy designed to "civilize" Native Americans. They defined "civilized" people as those who possessed an agricultural economy and republican government; learned to read, write, and speak the English language; and adopted the Christian religion. Washington believed that unless the Cherokees and other Indians became "civilized," they would not be able to survive; thus, he viewed his policy of destroying native cultures as humanitarian. Washington and other officials also had an ulterior motive: they hoped that if Indians adopted the life-style of frontier farmers, they would be willing to cede additional land used for hunting—land that could be opened to white settlement.

The first step in the process of "civilization" was to convince Indians to move out of their traditional towns and settle on isolated homesteads. Many Cherokees whose towns had been destroyed during the wars of the eighteenth century complied at least in part because they recognized how vulnerable their towns were to invading armies. Because the Cherokees held land in common, an Indian family could clear and occupy any unused land; thus, pioneer farms began to dot the Cherokee landscape.

White agents whom Washington appointed to live among the Cherokees introduced the technology of European culture. They taught Cherokee men, contrary to the aboriginal division of labor, how to fence fields and plow. They instructed women in the use of cotton cards, spinning wheels, and looms. In addition, the United States government employed blacksmiths and established gristmills.

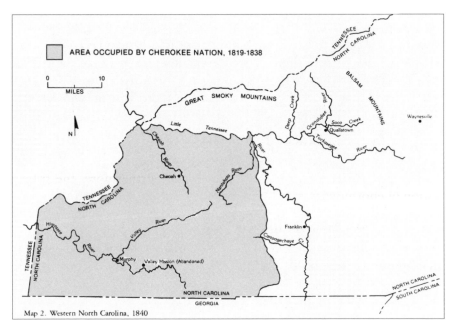

Map 2. Western North Carolina, 1840

Shown in this map is the area of extreme western North Carolina occupied by the Cherokee Nation, 1819–1838. From John R. Finger, *The Eastern Band of Cherokees, 1819–1900* (Knoxville: University of Tennessee Press, 1984) 30; reproduced courtesy University of Tennessee Press.

Many Cherokees welcomed the United States government's "civilization" program. Recognizing the impossibility of maintaining a hunting and trading economy with their diminished land base, they saw commercial agriculture as the tribe's economic salvation. Some Cherokees, particularly those living in northern Georgia and Alabama, became quite wealthy with the aid and encouragement of the United States government. By 1835, for example, Joseph Vann was operating an enormous plantation with the labor of more than a hundred slaves, a tavern on the federal road that ran through the Cherokee Nation, and a steamboat on the Tennessee River. Literate in English and a patron of a nearby Protestant mission school, Vann lived in an elegant mansion with white columns and tasteful furnishings. By white standards, the Cherokee Joseph Vann was clearly a "civilized" man.

Cherokee leaders, in particular, favored the "civilization" program because they believed that an English education would enable the next generation of leadership to protect the Cherokee homeland more effectively. Far too often, Indians had lost their land because they did not understand the white man's language or law. Education promised at least

41

some protection. The leaders also believed that a cultural transformation would enable them to survive and hold on to their land by counteracting white prejudice against them. The dominant white image of the Indian as a bloodthirsty savage gave rise to fear and hatred. The Cherokees hoped that if they became culturally indistinguishable from whites, they would no longer be perceived as a dangerous threat. Whites might then permit them to live peacefully in their ancestral homeland.

For this reason, the Cherokee chiefs permitted Moravian missionaries to build a school in northern Georgia in 1800. The Cherokees were not particularly interested in Christianity—the Moravians preached for almost a decade before making their first Cherokee convert—but they eagerly sought admission to the school. The Moravians, as well as the Baptists, Methodists, and Congregationalists who later joined them in the Cherokee mission field, viewed Christianity and "civilization" as intrinsically linked. In order to convert and "civilize" Cherokee children, all denominations except the Methodists operated boarding schools so that children could be removed from the corrupting influence of their parents. In addition to reading, writing, and arithmetic, students at the boarding schools learned the "arts of civilized life." Missionaries taught boys how to plow and chop wood and girls how to cook, sew, and keep house. They also set aside time each day for reading the Bible, singing hymns, and praying. Some Cherokee students proved so capable academically that they went to New England for additional education.

In the 1820s young men who had received an English education began to enter responsible positions in Cherokee government. Although the Cherokees had been recording their laws since 1808, this new generation of leadership believed that they needed a more formal political system and a more centralized government in order to protect both their own private property and their nation's territory. In response the Cherokees built a national capital, New Echota, in north Georgia and called a convention to write a constitution. The constitution of 1827 closely resembled that of the United States: it provided for the separation of executive, legislative, and judicial powers and for a system of checks and balances.

John Ross, who became chief in an election held according to the provisions of this constitution, was the epitome of the leadership of the Cherokee Nation in this period. Not only did Ross read and write English but he also spoke the language more fluently than he did Cherokee. He was a wealthy planter and owned several stores in the Nation. He also was a Cherokee patriot, intensely proud of his people's accomplishments and zealous in defense of their rights.

Two of the most notable residents of the Cherokee Nation were John Ross (*left*), a wealthy planter and merchant who was elected chief of the Nation, and Sequoyah (also known as George Guess), who created a method of expressing the Cherokee language in writing. Watercolor portraits reproduced in Thomas L. McKenney and James Hall, *The Indian Tribes of North America* (Edinburgh: John Grant, 3 volumes, 1933–1934), 3, facing 312, and 1, facing 130, respectively.

The Cherokee government actively promoted education and "civilization" among the Cherokees. Sequoyah, a Cherokee who knew no English but realized that literacy was a genuine advantage, developed a way of writing Cherokee in the early 1820s. His syllabary of eighty-five symbols, one for each sound, aided the nation's "civilization" effort. The government purchased a printing press and types in the syllabary, established a newspaper, and appointed as editor Elias Boudinot, a New England-educated Cherokee. In 1828 Boudinot published the first issue of the *Cherokee Phoenix*, which printed news, the laws of the Cherokee Nation, editorials, and Bible passages in English and Cherokee. The government also made plans for a museum and an institution of higher education.

Cherokee accomplishments did nothing, however, to diminish white demands for their land. The discovery of gold in the Cherokee Nation in 1828 increased the pressure on state and federal governments to obtain Cherokee land for white settlement. The state of Georgia was particularly insistent. In 1802 the federal government had promised to extinguish Indian land titles within the state in exchange for Georgia's cession of western lands, which would become the states of Alabama and Mississippi. In the late 1820s Georgia demanded that the federal government fulfill its promise. When the old Indian fighter Andrew Jackson became president in 1829, the state's position gained support in Washington.

By established practice, the federal government could not merely seize Indian land: federal officials were obliged to negotiate a treaty under which the Cherokees would exchange their land in the Southeast for territory west of the Mississippi River. The Cherokees, however, refused to discuss the matter. Georgia tried to force them into negotiating by enacting a series of laws that abolished the Cherokee government, denied the Cherokees basic civil rights such as the right to testify in court, and distributed Cherokee land within the state to whites through a lottery. The Cherokees suffered enormously, but they nevertheless refused to negotiate. Finally, in 1835, a small, unauthorized group of men signed a removal treaty. The Cherokees protested the treaty, and John Ross collected more than 15,000 signatures (representing almost the entire population) on a petition requesting the United States Senate to withhold ratification. The Senate, however, approved the treaty by a margin of one vote in the spring of 1836.

The treaty gave the Cherokees two years to vacate their homeland and go west to present-day Oklahoma. By the summer of 1838 few Cherokees had prepared to move, so the president dispatched United States soldiers, who rounded people up and placed them in stockades. Ross appealed to the president to permit his people to delay removal until winter, when water and game would be more plentiful en route. President Martin Van Buren, who had succeeded Jackson in 1837, relented, and late in 1838 the Cherokees moved west. Of the 16,000 who traveled the "Trail of Tears," about 4,000 died.

Not all Cherokees went west. Scattered families remained in Tennessee, Georgia, and Alabama, and in North Carolina an entire Indian community, known as the Oconaluftee Cherokees, managed to avoid removal. The Oconaluftees were among the most conservative people in the Cherokee Nation. They preferred their own council house and chief, the old religion, and a traditional education to the centralized government, Christianity, and mission schools advocated by the Nation's leaders. So indifferent were these Cherokees to the Nation's cultural transformation that when the Cherokee government ceded all territory east of the Little Tennessee River in 1819, they chose to withdraw from the Nation. Receiving individual tracts of land, the Oconaluftee Cherokees regarded themselves as citizens of the state of North Carolina. Therefore, the treaty by which the Cherokee Nation relinquished its land in the East did not apply to the Oconaluftee Cherokees.

When soldiers began imprisoning Cherokees slated for removal, the Oconaluftees found themselves in an awkward situation. They had considerable sympathy for Indians who hid from the soldiers, but they feared that any effort to aid the fugitives might jeopardize their own relatively secure position. Tension increased when Tsali, a citizen of the Cherokee Nation, and his sons killed two soldiers and fled to the mountains. Euchella, a Cherokee whose status was in question, and a small group of Cherokees ultimately captured and executed Tsali. As a reward for their services the United States commander permitted Euchella's band to join the Oconaluftees. These two groups, plus the few Cherokees who escaped the soldiers, came to be known as the Eastern Band of Cherokee Indians. Although his death had little to do with the right of the Oconaluftee Cherokees to remain in North Carolina, Tsali soon became a folk hero and a symbol not only of opposition to removal but also of the traditional Cherokee life-style and values.

Because of conflicting claims to the land the Oconaluftees received in 1819, the state of North Carolina decided to buy the Indians' title. William Holland Thomas, a local trader, acted as the Indians' agent and purchased a number of other tracts for the Oconaluftees in the years preceding the Civil War. When the war began, Thomas, who was an ardent secessionist, convinced the Cherokees to provide soldiers for the Confederacy. After the war, Thomas's health failed, and the Cherokees faced a major crisis. Thomas had neglected to deed to the Cherokees some land for which they actually had paid. His financial affairs were in shambles, and his creditors seized, along with Thomas's own assets, land that in fact belonged to the Cherokees. In addition, the Cherokees had difficulty paying their property taxes, and county sheriffs threatened to sell their land in order to collect delinquent levies. Fearing that the Cherokees would lose their land base, the federal government eventually stepped in and decided to hold the land in trust for the Indians to prevent their being cheated out of it. Therefore, Qualla Boundary, the Cherokee reservation, was not land given to the Indians but land they bought.

In the years after the Civil War, the Cherokees continued to live a fairly traditional way of life. Most spoke only Cherokee, and many read the Sequoyah syllabary, which parents taught children at home. The federal government provided educational opportunities only sporadically. In the 1880s, however, Quakers from Indiana established day schools in several communities and a boarding school in the town of Cherokee. Like earlier missionaries, they attempted to eradicate traditional practices and beliefs. Among other things, they forced children to speak English, and many Indians began to abandon their native tongue.

Chief Nimrod Jarrett Smith was instrumental in obtaining for the Oconaluftee Cherokees a corporate charter that enabled the group to transact business, plead cases in court, and ultimately to exist as a recognized political unit. Photograph (ca. 1890) from *Eleventh Census of the United States: Extra Census Bulletin* (Washington, D.C.: Government Printing Office, 1892).

The Cherokees in this period had a rather tenuous legal status. Although governed by a chief and council, they constituted neither a county nor a town, entities recognized by state law, because they lived in four counties and several distinct townships. Therefore, in 1889 Chief Nimrod Jarrett Smith obtained for the Oconaluftees a corporate charter similar to those for businesses, and the Eastern Band of Cherokee Indians became a corporation. This charter permitted the tribe to transact business and take cases to court and was later amended to enable the band to act as a bona fide political unit.

During this period, many whites in western North Carolina became envious of the Indians' resources and benefits. As a result, the Eastern Band was inundated by whites who wanted to get on the tribal roll, or list of recognized Cherokees, in order to share in proceeds from the sale of timber on tribal land and in a rumored division of the band's communally owned territory. This dramatic increase in population severely strained the resources of the Eastern Band, and by the Great Depression of the 1930s the Cherokees were suffering acutely.

In the 1930s the United States government initiated a number of programs to help the Cherokees. A new school staffed by federally paid teachers offered children a better education. Scientific farming techniques and the construction of modern housing improved the lives

Shown at top is a typical Cherokee log cabin and farmstead, ca. 1890. The woman at right is pounding corn into meal. In the photograph at bottom a teacher and her students pose in front of a training school in 1893. Photograph at top from Negative No. 1000-A, Smithsonian Institution, National Anthropological Archives; at bottom courtesy Museum of the Cherokee Indian.

This Cherokee family was photographed at the Cherokee Reservation in western North Carolina ca. 1936. From *State*, 4 (October 24, 1936), 7.

of many Cherokees. The government also helped Indian craftsmen organize a cooperative to market their baskets, pottery, wood carvings, and other items.

The Cherokees attracted government attention in part because of the development of the Great Smoky Mountains National Park on land adjoining Qualla Boundary. The opening of the park in 1934 brought thousands of tourists to Cherokee, the Indian town at the eastern entrance. After World War II the stream swelled to a flood, causing the tourist economy on the reservation to thrive in the 1960s and 1970s. In order to attract tourist dollars, the Cherokees often had to provide visitors with a stereotypical view of Indian culture, including teepees and warbonnets, which Cherokees did not use traditionally. The successful production of the outdoor drama *Unto These Hills*, a romanticized account of the legend of Tsali, also drew visitors. At the same time, other more culturally authentic attractions were also popular with tourists. The Cherokee Museum, the Qualla Arts and Crafts cooperative, and Oconaluftee Indian Village, an authentic reproduction of an eighteenth century village, attracted visitors from across the country. The Cherokees were no longer an isolated people.

In order to attract tourist dollars, the Cherokees often had to provide visitors with a stereotypical view of Indian culture through teepees and elaborate warbonnets, which were not part of the traditional Cherokee heritage. Photograph (1945) courtesy of the North Carolina Office of Archives and History.

Despite the success of the tourist economy in the postwar years, the Cherokees faced an economic crisis in the 1980s. New tourist attractions in western North Carolina and eastern Tennessee, such as the Dollywood theme-park, began to siphon valuable tourist dollars away from the reservation. Moreover, the Reagan administration cut federal programs for Native Americans in an effort to control the exploding budget deficit. The combination of increased competition for tourist dollars and federal spending cuts decimated the Qualla Boundary economy. In 1990, the per capita income on the reservation was about $7,000, and more than one-third of Cherokee families lived below the poverty line. In the winter, when the tourist economy completely shut down, unemployment could reach 40 percent in the town of Cherokee.

With wintertime unemployment often reaching 40 percent, the Cherokee tribal elders turned to gaming to provide steady employment and a regular revenue stream. In November 1997, the opening of Harrah's Cherokee Casino on the Qualla Boundary was an immediate success. One-half of all profits from the casino are distributed to enrolled Cherokees, while the other half funds tribal projects. Photograph courtesy of the Harrah's Cherokee Casino and Hotel.

The Eastern Band of Cherokee Tribal Council approved a massive $633 million expansion for Harrah's Cherokee Casino and Hotel in January 2007. In addition to totally renovating all existing facilities, the expansion plans include construction of a luxury spa, a 3,000-seat theater, and a third hotel tower (depicted at left). Architect's rendering of the new hotel tower courtesy of the Harrah's Cherokee Casino and Hotel.

Another problem hindered economic development on the Qualla Boundary. Individual Cherokees did not hold deeds to the land they occupied, although they did have a possessory right to it. They could lease this right for twenty-five years to an outsider with the approval of the tribal government, or they could sell or will it to another Cherokee. No land could be sold without permission of the Cherokee Council and the president of the United States. Consequently, industrial and commercial establishments were reluctant to invest money on Qualla Boundary.

Given the economic problems of the 1980s, the Cherokee Tribal Council opted to pursue gaming on the reservation. The Cherokees already ran a successful bingo operation, but in 1988, the United States Congress passed the Indian Gaming Regulatory Act (IGRA). The IGRA came in the wake of a controversial Supreme Court decision (*Cabazon Band of Mission Indians v. California*) that held that states could not regulate gaming on federal Indian reservations. The IGRA established the blueprint for tribes seeking to open casinos on their lands and required state governors to negotiate "in good faith" with tribal governments. In 1994, despite resistance from within the Cherokee community, the Tribal Council voted 11-1 to pass a gaming ordinance. A few months later, Chief Jonathan Taylor signed a gaming compact with North Carolina governor Jim Hunt. The compact would allow the Cherokees to open a modern Las Vegas-style casino with video gaming machines on the Qualla Boundary. The Cherokee Tribal Council subsequently began asking for proposals from established casino corporations.

In November of 1997, Harrah's Cherokee Casino opened. It proved to be an immediate success. According to the contract with Harrah's, the tribe would receive 72.5 percent of the casino profits the first year. That number would increase in future years until it reached 83 percent. According to the ordinance passed by the Tribal Council, 50 percent of tribal profits would go directly to all enrolled Cherokees in the form of yearly per capita paychecks. The other half would be used to fund tribal projects. In the years since Harrah's opened, the Cherokees have used gaming profits to build a new wastewater treatment plant, remodel the museum, fund child-care programs, expand tribal recreational facilities, improve housing, and fund health-care programs. By 2007, the casino, which by then included a new fifteen-story hotel, employed 1,900, many of whom were Cherokee, making it the largest employer in North Carolina west of Asheville.

Despite the economic success, the casino remained a source of controversy both on the reservation and in the surrounding counties. Cherokee critics worried that it would lead to the destruction of traditional Cherokee culture, moral decay, crime, gambling addiction, and other social problems. Non-Cherokee critics in western North Carolina had similar concerns about how the casino would affect the region. Supporters, however, pointed to the new programs funded by gaming profits, some of which could be used to preserve Cherokee culture. "Why do people think that you have to be poor to preserve your culture," Cherokee Henry Lambert told an Atlanta reporter in 1998. "You can do a lot more to preserve your culture if you've got money." Moreover, the Tribal Council has used the success of the casino to try to recruit other businesses and industries to Cherokee. To other Cherokees, the casino was a necessary evil, a practical attempt to deal with the current economic problems. According to former chief Joyce Dugan, "gambling is our salvation. I don't like to admit that. But without it we'd be in real trouble."

Chapter 5

THE LUMBEEſ

The origin of the Lumbee Indians of Robeson County is far more obscure than that of the Cherokees, and their early history poses many puzzling questions. When European settlers first took notice, the Indians living along the Lumber River were speaking English, living in log cabins, dressing like whites, attending Baptist and Methodist churches, and farming small tracts of very poor land. Although they shared the same culture, whites recognized these Indians as a distinct ethnic group and, over the years, referred to them by a variety of names, including Scuffletonians, Croatans, Cherokees of Robeson County, Cheraws, and finally Lumbees. The Lumbee Indians are probably the descendants of coastal Indians who banded together after the decimation of their tribes. Because of differences in their own languages and customs and the relative proximity of whites, these people adopted the English pioneer way of life. Living in a swampy, undesirable area, the Lumbees managed to survive and to develop a distinct community held together by bonds of kinship.

Until the 1830s Lumbees enjoyed the privileges of citizenship, including the right to vote and bear arms. In the wake of the Nat Turner rebellion, however, the state of North Carolina enacted a new constitution in 1835 aimed at controlling nonwhites and preventing slave insurrections. The constitution prohibited "persons of color" from voting, serving on juries, testifying against whites, bearing arms, and learning to read and write. While the constitution did not specifically mention the Lumbees, subsequent court decisions applied these measures to them as well as African Americans. Because the Lumbees could no longer exercise basic civil rights, they became targets of unscrupulous whites who defrauded many of them of the small amount of land they held and forced them to provide free labor.

When the Civil War began, the Lumbees were excluded from military service because they were not white. The Confederacy did, however, attempt to exploit Lumbee labor in the construction of forts along the lower Cape Fear River. In 1862 a yellow fever epidemic struck the region and resulted in a serious labor shortage. Planters objected to the use of their expensive slaves for such unhealthy work, so

Henry Berry Lowry, leader of a band of Lumbee exiles who rebelled at Confederate rule and later conducted a series of guerrilla-style raids from their home in the swamps of Robeson County, is regarded as history's most famous Lumbee. His mysterious disappearance in 1872 added to the legendary qualities of his life and exploits. Photograph from Adolph I. Dial and David K. Elides, *The Only Land I Know: A History of the Lumbee Indians* (San Francisco: Indian Historian Press, 1975), 42.

authorities began to draft the Lumbees to build the fortifications. The Lumbees objected, and many men hid in the swamps in order to avoid conscription for labor. In the swamps, they encountered a number of Union soldiers who had escaped from the Confederate prison at Florence, South Carolina. Gradually, the Lumbees became a pro–Union enclave in the Confederate South.

Many Lumbee men could not come out of the swamps to farm because of the threat of conscription, and their families began to suffer severely. At the same time, wealthy planters in Robeson County prospered. Not only did the planters have slaves to farm for them, but they also enjoyed an exemption from military service offered to owners of more than twenty slaves. The Lumbees as well as other poor people in Robeson County resented the privileges of the well-to-do.

In 1864 Henry Berry Lowry, a sixteen-year-old Lumbee, and two brothers allegedly stole some hogs from a wealthy planter and took them to their father's home, where the family shared them with escaped Union soldiers. The following day the planter discovered hogs' ears bearing his mark on the Lowry farm. Although the planter did not press charges, he subsequently directed conscription officials to the Lowry family. Henry Berry and his brothers retaliated by ambushing the planter and fleeing to the swamps. Less than a month later, they killed the local conscription officer. From this point on, the Lowry band was at war with the Confederacy. In a daring assault on the Robeson County Courthouse in Lumberton, they seized guns and ammunition and

An artist for a popular American pictorial magazine made this sketch of the Lowry band in 1872. By that time the Lowrys had attracted nationwide attention. Engraving from *Harper's Weekly*, 16 (March 30, 1872), 249.

conducted a series of raids on prosperous plantations but carefully spared small farms. The Lowrys' attacks on the privileged and their willingness to share the provisions they stole generated considerable support for them among poor African Americans, whites, and Indians in Robeson County.

The North Carolina Home Guard, the local Confederate militia, conducted a sweep of Lumbee farms in the spring of 1865 hoping, but failing, to capture Henry Berry Lowry and his band. At the home of Henry Berry's father the militia found the gold head of a cane that had been stolen from a wealthy planter. They arrested the entire household and led them to a nearby plantation, where a makeshift trial was held. The Home Guard convicted Henry Berry's father and one of his brothers, took them into the woods, and executed them. By the next day, Union forces under the command of Gen. William T. Sherman were advancing on Robeson County, and the Home Guard released the remaining prisoners.

The Lumbees looked forward to the arrival of Union forces, and many of them provided assistance to the soldiers. As Union sympathizers, they believed that Sherman would liberate them from the oppression of the large Confederate landowners. Unfortunately, Sherman's troops did not distinguish clearly between friends and foe in carrying out the

This view of the Henry Berry Lowry house was made ca. 1975; the house had then undergone only minor alterations since the time it was occupied by Lowry and his family. The 1865 execution of Lowry's father and brother took place only a few hundred yards from the house. Photograph by William P. Revels; reproduced from Dial and Eliades, *The Only Land I Know*, 60.

general's scorched earth policy, and they took food and livestock belonging to rebel planters and loyal Lumbees alike. When the soldiers moved north, they left the Lumbees in more serious economic straits than before; and the Lowry band continued to steal in order to feed itself and its families. Gradually, the number of the band increased as the Lumbees fled from white harassment stemming from anger over the Indians' Unionist sympathies.

The end of the war was expected to vindicate the loyal Lumbees, secure their civil rights, and elevate their social status. Unfortunately, Union victory did not extend to the Lowry band. Immediately after the war, Conservatives, as former Confederates came to be called, remained in power and relentlessly pursued the Lumbee outlaws. By 1868 Radicals in the United States Congress, who might have been expected to support the Lumbee cause, had assumed control of Reconstruction, and the Republican Party, of which the Radicals were part, dominated North Carolina politics. The Lumbees, who supported Republicans, looked to the new government to punish members of the Home Guard who had killed Indians. Republicans, however, claimed that legal technicalities prevented their bringing members of the Home Guard to trial. Actually, they believed that such trials were politically inexpedient.

The Lumbees were also disappointed that Republican officeholders would not permit Henry Berry Lowry and his followers to return to their homes and families. The Republicans, the Indians hoped, would regard the Lowry band as Unionist guerrillas who struggled against the Confederacy. Instead, the Republicans decided that the Lowrys were common criminals who stole for economic rather than political reasons. The Republicans adopted this view in part because they did not want to be associated with the kind of vigilante violence of which they accused the Conservative Democrats and the Ku Klux Klan. The result of this decision was a split in the Republican Party of Robeson County and the election of Conservative Democrats. The decision also condemned Henry Berry Lowry and his band to the swamps of the Lumber River and Robeson County and to years of exile and violence.

In the late 1860s and 1870s the exploits of Henry Berry Lowry established him as a legendary figure. He stole from the rich and gave to the poor, made daring escapes from jail, and liberated members of his band who had been captured. Thanks to information provided by relatives and friends, he always seemed to know the location of the militia—but the militia could not find him. He staged surprise attacks and ambushes and then disappeared into the swamps. One of his most remarkable feats occurred in July 1871. A company of militiamen had been rounding up wives of the Lowry band to hold as hostages. Having sent the hostages to headquarters, eighteen members of the company paused for a break at Wire Grass Landing in Robeson County. They noticed a canoe coming toward them on the river and recognized the lone occupant as Henry Berry Lowry. The militia opened fire. Instead of retreating, Lowry jumped into the water on the opposite side of the canoe and, using the boat as a shield, began swimming toward the militia while he fired his gun over the side. The militia ultimately withdrew with their wounded. Lowry had triumphed once again. He subsequently secured the release of the women by threatening to capture white women and take them to the swamps, a threat that whites in Robeson County took very seriously.

In February 1872, the Lowry band robbed a store in Lumberton. Instead of taking food, as was their custom, they also absconded with a safe containing $22,000. This was the Lowry band's last raid, and Henry Berry never again appeared in public. During the following year, other members of the band disappeared or met violent deaths, carrying with them to their graves the secret of their leader's whereabouts. Had he escaped the country with the money he took on his last raid? Had he drowned in the swamps? Had he been shot accidentally by one of his own men? Rumors circulated, but no explanation was ever substantiated; indeed, the mystery of Henry Berry Lowry's fate has never been resolved.

Henry Berry Lowry's mysterious disappearance contributed to his heroic image. Certainly, he was a remarkable man. He struggled against injustice, and he helped preserve the ethnic identity of his people. Before Lowry, the Lumbees had been poor and powerless. Regarding the Lumbees and African Americans as racially inferior, whites denied them equal protection of the law. The courageous exploits of the Lowry band instilled in the Indians a sense of pride and a confidence in their ability to control their lives. White North Carolinians gradually recognized that the Lumbees would not readily accept oppression. In the late nineteenth century, whites began to appreciate the Indian ancestry of the Lumbees, although their racist attitudes toward nonwhites remained fixed.

Following Reconstruction, institutionalized racial segregation emerged in North Carolina. In most of the South, Jim Crow segregation meant a biracial society; but in Robeson County, as well as elsewhere in eastern North Carolina, segregation was triracial (black, white, Indian). The state legislature recognized the Indians of Robeson County as "Croatans," the name of the tribe associated with Sir Walter Raleigh's Lost Colony, and established separate schools for them. The need for teachers prompted the legislature to appropriate $500 in 1887 for the establishment near Pembroke of the Croatan Normal School (normal schools specialized in training teachers). No money was provided for a building, but the Lumbees rallied to the cause of education and erected a two-story building in time for school to open in the fall. The name of the school changed several times, and it is presently known as the University of North Carolina, Pembroke (UNCP). In 2005, Gov. Michael F. Easley signed a bill recognizing UNCP, which is part of the University of North Carolina system, as a historically Indian university. The Lumbees have also had several different names and acquired their current designation in 1953.

The Lumbees did not oppose segregation in the late nineteenth and early twentieth centuries. Instead, they welcomed an opportunity to develop an Indian consciousness and to manage their own affairs. Indian churches established a Baptist Association and a Methodist Conference separate from white and "colored" organizations. An Indian school committeeman directed the Lumbee educational system, and a local leader bargained with the white political establishment in the county to acquire public services for the Indian community.

(*Above*) The first building occupied by the Indian Normal School near Pembroke in Robeson County was constructed by Lumbees in 1887. The school, with an initial enrollment of fifteen, served as the principal educational facility for the Lumbees until 1909. (*Below*) Prospect School was an all-Indian public school in Robeson County. This view of the facility and its student body was made about 1930. Both photographs courtesy Elmer Hunt; reproduced from Dial and Eliades, *The Only Land I Know*, 92, 161, respectively.

Although racial segregation did help engender an Indian identity that had earlier been assailed, exclusion from white institutions and full participation in the political process denied Indians opportunities and real control of their lives. Segregation made them second-class citizens. Until 1947, for example, the residents of Pembroke, most of whom were Lumbees, could not elect their own mayor. Instead, the governor of North Carolina appointed white men to serve as mayor of this Indian town. Furthermore, many restaurants in Robeson County denied service to the Lumbees as well as to African Americans, and some establishments had three water fountains—one for each race—and six bathrooms—one for each race and sex.

The civil rights movement of the 1950s encouraged many Lumbees to struggle against discrimination. In January of 1958 the Ku Klux Klan, which opposed equal rights for African Americans and Indians, held a rally near Maxton in Robeson County. The Lumbees remembered that in 1870 Henry Berry Lowry had killed the local leader of the despised Klan, and in the tradition of Lowry, they went armed to the rally determined to break it up. They succeeded. As soon as the Lumbees fired their guns into the air, the Klan, heavily outnumbered, fled across the state line into South Carolina and never returned publicly to Robeson County with its message of racial hatred.

The "Indian Uprising of Robeson County," as one eyewitness called it, attracted national media attention. Several reporters and photographers were present that cold, wintry night. *Time, Newsweek, Life*, the *New York Times*, the *Washington Post*, and other major daily and weekly news publications published articles and photographs describing how the Lumbee Indians of Robeson County routed the racist Klan. Although the stories often employed racist and ethnocentric language—writers often used terms such as "redskin," "war-whoops," and "scalping"— most reporters and editors praised the Lumbees for standing up to the Klan. A few Lumbee leaders were even interviewed on national television. Consequently, the Lumbees, for the first time since the days of Henry Berry Lowry, became well known outside of eastern North Carolina.

As the national civil rights movement escalated, the Lumbees continued to demand their civil rights in Robeson County. In 1972 they challenged the practice of "double voting." The immediate issue was the election of members to the county school board. The population of Lumberton, the county seat, was overwhelmingly white, and children in Lumberton attended schools supervised by a city school board. The majority of the children who went to schools governed by the Robeson

60

In January 1958, the Ku Klux Klan held a rally near the Robeson County town of Maxton. Local Lumbee Indians responded by interrupting the rally and firing guns into the air, completely routing the Klan from the area. At the conclusion of the Lumbee "raid," the Indians burned the Klan's grand wizard in effigy. Photography from Lew Barton, *The Most Ironic Story in American History* (Charlotte: Associated Printing Corporation, 1967), following 142.

County school board were Indian, yet prior to 1972 the majority of the county school board was white. This situation existed because residents of Lumberton also voted for the county school board, which possessed no authority over Lumberton schools. So long as this "double voting" continued, Indians could not control their children's education. The Lumbees thereupon took the matter to court. The Indians won their case, and "double voting" ended. By 1974 a majority of the Robeson school board and the superintendent of county schools were Lumbees.

During the 1970s, the Lumbees also exposed racial bias in the hiring of county employees and in the county's judicial system, which convicted 96 percent of Indians accused of crimes but found only 28 percent of white defendants guilty. In February of 1988, two local Indian men stormed the offices of the *Robesonian*, a newspaper in Lumberton, to focus state and national attention on racism and discrimination in the county. After several tense hours, the two men surrendered to agents from the Federal Bureau of Investigation after representatives from the governor's office promised to look into the matter, a promise they failed to keep.

Along with attacking racial injustice, the Lumbees continued to seek full federal acknowledgment in the 1970s. In 1956, the United States Congress had passed a bill recognizing the Lumbees as Indians; but the bill, written during a time when the United States government was trying to terminate its relationship with Indian nations, also denied them tribal sovereignty and excluded them from most federal programs for Native Americans. In the 1970s, federal Indian policy shifted from termination to self-determination, which offered recognized Native Americans more sovereignty. Moreover, the United States government initiated new programs offering Indians much needed assistance. Consequently, a number of unrecognized tribes, including the Lumbees, sought full acknowledgment. In 1978, the Bureau of Indian Affairs (BIA) established the Federal Acknowledgment Process (FAP), a set of specific guidelines for federal recognition of a Native American tribe, to handle these applications. Using the FAP as a blueprint, the Lumbees spent $1.5 million in the 1980s compiling a two-volume petition that included thousands of supporting documents. The BIA, however, declined to consider the Lumbee petition on the grounds that the 1956 legislation prohibited such consideration. Broken, but not defeated, the Lumbees continued their pursuit of full federal recognition in the late twentieth century, opting to work through the United States Congress rather than the BIA. For most of the 1990s and early 2000s, the Lumbees faced opposition from several powerful North Carolina politicians, some of whom feared that the tribe might open a casino like the one in Cherokee in southeastern North Carolina. Moreover, other federal tribes also opposed the Lumbees, fearing that officially recognizing the tribe, which had approximately 50,000 enrolled members, would dilute the already scarce funds for Native American programs. But in 2009, a bill offering full federal recognition to the Lumbees passed the United States House of Representatives and was sent to the Senate for consideration in 2010.

From the exploits of Henry Berry Lowry in the Civil War era, to the routing of the Klan in the 1950s, to the aggressive pursuit of full acknowledgment in the late twentieth and early twenty-first centuries, the Lumbees have signaled their determination to participate fully in the economic, political, and social life of Robeson County. From remnants of extirpated tribes that relied in part on anonymity in order to survive, the Lumbees became in the course of the twentieth and early twenty-first centuries an Indian people with a strong group identity. At the same time, they emerged as a powerful force for racial equality.

Chapter 6

NATIVE CAROLINIANS TODAY

The Cherokees and Lumbees are not the only American Indians in North Carolina. By the turn of the twenty-first century, there were more than 100,000 Native Americans living in the Tar Heel State, the largest indigenous population in any state east of the Mississippi River. The Eastern Band of Cherokee Indians, the only federally recognized tribe in North Carolina, numbered approximately 13,000. The majority of other Tar Heel Native Americans were members of state recognized tribes. The Haliwa-Saponis (3,500) lived primarily in Halifax and Warren counties; the Coharies (1,200) in Sampson and Harnett counties; the Waccamaw-Siouans (3,000) in Bladen and Columbus counties; the Sapponis (400) in Person County; the Meherrins (600) in Hertford County; and the Occaneechi-Saponis (1,000) in Alamance and Orange counties. Approximately 45,000 Lumbees lived in and around Robeson County, as did a few thousand Tuscaroras, who were related to the Lumbees but claimed a separate tribal identity and had not been recognized by North Carolina.

For most Native Americans in North Carolina, especially those in the central and eastern regions of the state, their origins resembled the history of the Lumbees. By the end of the mid-eighteenth century, European settlement had spread across the Piedmont. Small tribes, mostly Siouan, fled before the massive invasion of whites. Most Indians joined their kinsmen in eastern and southern North Carolina, southern Virginia, and South Carolina. To escape complete annihilation and confrontation with whites, these survivors of the once large Indian population of eastern North Carolina moved onto marginal lands, largely undesirable to whites. It is from these last surviving groups that most native Carolinians trace their ancestry.

In the nineteenth and early twentieth centuries, the small Indian groups in central and eastern North Carolina confronted many of the same problems as the Lumbees. Classified as nonwhites by the dominant white society, Indians suffered the effects of racial segregation as they struggled to preserve their communities and their Indian identity. County school boards usually denied Indians admission to white schools. In 1885 the North Carolina legislature mandated separate schools for the

Lumbees but ignored the educational needs of other Indians. Whites normally insisted that Indians attend schools established for African Americans. Most Indians refused to enroll in black schools, in part, perhaps, because of their own racial prejudice, but primarily because they feared that official designation as "colored" would destroy their own ethnic identity and result in further discrimination. In addition, county governments typically allocated far less funding for black schools than for white schools, and, consequently, children who attended those schools usually received an inferior education.

In a number of Indian communities, parents struggled to provide separate Indian schools for their children. Many of these were subscription schools to which students paid monthly fees. Native Americans who wanted to improve educational opportunities for their people sometimes encountered open hostility from whites. In 1910 an Indian teacher at a state-supported black school tried to establish a separate school for Haliwa-Saponi children. He lost his job, and the Haliwa-Saponis had to wait almost fifty years for their own school.

The Waccamaws had a somewhat better experience. In 1891 the Waccamaws organized a school committee and built a one-room schoolhouse. Families paid $40 per year to hire a teacher. Because they were so poor, the Waccamaws could not always raise the necessary funds, and the school operated sporadically. In the early twentieth century the state agreed to pay a teacher, but because the one assigned to the school was African American, Indian parents preferred to see the school close. In the 1920s the school reopened with Indian teachers educated at Indian State Normal School in Pembroke. A decade later, Bladen County offered to pay the teachers if the Waccamaws provided classrooms. The Native Americans constructed a building with materials from a razed white school, and by the early 1940s two hundred students from Columbus and Bladen counties attended a school there. Conditions at the school left much to be desired. In 1950 James Evan Alexander described the school in an article in *The American Indian*:

The present school is inadequate. It is poorly constructed, drafty, overcrowded, lacking in books and desks, and portions of it have never been ceiled on the inside. Bare studs in the room add to the general dismal appearance. There are no cloak rooms; no entry halls. Access to certain rooms are only through another. No playground or playground equipment. Three of the rooms have an ordinary tin, wood heater. The fourth is provided with no heat at all. Its construction, as well as lack of exits, create an extremely dangerous fire hazard. There is no fire fighting equipment or extinguishers. The only source of water is a hand pumped well which requires priming.

Four teachers instructed students through the eighth grade. In order to attend high school, students had to leave home. Few did so, and the educational level of most remained low. Nevertheless, the Waccamaws were justifiably proud of their school and dismayed when Bladen officials classified it as "white" on their list of county schools.

In 1942 the East Carolina Indian School was established in Sampson County. A consolidated school, offering instruction in grades one through twelve, it served the Indian people of Sampson and surrounding counties. Because of inadequate facilities for Indian education elsewhere, high school students from Harnett, Bladen, Columbus, Cumberland, and Person counties also attended, boarding with local Indian families. Neither the county nor the state, however, provided sufficient funding for the Indian school. Parents often donated labor, supplies, and salaries for art and music teachers at the same time they petitioned state and county educational authorities for such basic needs as a dormitory, a gymnasium, a lunchroom, and fully equipped science laboratories. When the Sampson County schools were integrated in 1965, the East Carolina Indian School closed.

Separate Indian schools disappeared in the 1960s when North Carolina racially integrated its schools. Integration, however, brought new problems for Native Americans. An Indian teacher in Sampson County asked a reporter, "How would you like it if you were going to a school and you were the only one of your race there?" This often happened to children from the smaller Indian communities. Not only did they face social discrimination, but these children also risked losing their identity as Indians. Fortunately, sensitive teachers in some schools attempted to preserve the ethnic identity of Native American children and encouraged understanding on the part of non-Indians by developing special programs that focused on Indian heritage.

Native Carolinians emphasized education because they believed that it promised a brighter future for their children. In many cases, however, economic opportunities were limited. In the rural counties where most Native Americans lived, few high-paying jobs existed, and those that did went to whites instead of Indians. For many, the only way to survive was sharecropping. Under this system, a landowner permitted an Indian to farm a small tract of land on the condition that he receive a percentage of the Indian's crop. The percentage increased if the owner furnished seed, equipment, or other supplies. The sharecropper often had so little at the end of the year that he had to borrow once again from the owner, causing an unbroken cycle of debt.

Some Indians managed to hold on to their own land into the twentieth century, but individual whites, corporations, and even government officials constantly sought opportunities to seize native property. The loss of land by the Waccamaws provides a good example. In the 1920s a surveyor employed by the state of North Carolina traveled through the eastern counties locating "vacant" land, that is, land to which no recorded deed existed. The Native Americans, of course, had been living on the land long before deeds existed; but according to white officials, they did not have legal titles. The surveyor, who was also an agent for timber companies, claimed thousands of acres of "vacant" land for the state and promptly sold it to timber companies. North Carolina received the money from the sale, while the surveyor realized a commission from the timber companies. Many American Indians were forced off land they had occupied for years. Finally, descendants of a Waccamaw whose land was sold in this transaction sued. In 1963 the North Carolina Supreme Court awarded the descendants title to 126 acres. This case gave other Waccamaws hope.

Only gradually did the North Carolina government officially become cognizant of its Native American population. In 1889, four years after directing the establishment of Lumbee schools, the legislature granted the Cherokees a corporate charter and in 1913 designated another group of native Carolinians "Indians of Person County." Nevertheless, the state did little to address the problems of Indian people until the second half of the twentieth century. In 1953 the legislature finally extended official recognition to the Lumbees as an Indian tribe. State recognition came to the Haliwa-Saponis in 1965, the Waccamaw-Siouans in 1971, the Coharies in 1971, the Meherrins in 1986, the Sapponis in 1997, and the Occaneechi-Saponis in 2002.

In the second half of the twentieth century, an increasing number of North Carolina Indians moved out of their rural home communities and into urban areas. Pushed off small farms and out of blue-collar jobs by the changing economy in eastern North Carolina, Native Americans relocated to cities such as Charlotte, Greensboro, Raleigh, and Fayetteville to find new jobs. As the number of young Indians earning college degrees increased, many left their home towns and settled in metropolitan areas to find professional occupations. In order to adjust to the dramatic economic and social change, urban Native Americans formed intertribal development associations and organizations, including the Metrolina Native American Association of Charlotte; the Guilford Native American Association of Greensboro; the Cumberland County Association of Indian People in Fayetteville; and the Triangle

This family of Indians was photographed in Person County ca. 1948. Native Carolinians who reside in the county are presently recognized as "Indians of Person County." Photograph from *State*, 16 (February 12, 1949), 3.

Native American Society, which served Indian people in Raleigh, Durham, and Chapel Hill. These organizations offered their members job training, daycare, housing assistance, and a variety of other services.

In 1971 the North Carolina General Assembly established the North Carolina Commission of Indian Affairs (NCCIA). In 1977, the NCCIA became part of the North Carolina Department of Administration. According to the charter:

The purposes of the Commission shall be to deal fairly and effectively with Indian affairs: to bring local, state, and federal resources into focus for the implementation or continuation of meaningful programs for Indian citizens of the State of North Carolina; to provide aid and protection for Indians as needs are demonstrated; to prevent undue hardships; to assist Indian communities in social and economic development; and to promote recognition of and the right of Indians to pursue cultural and religious traditions considered by them to be sacred and meaningful to Native Americans.

The NCCIA consisted of representatives from the Eastern Band of Cherokee Indians, the state's recognized tribes, and the aforementioned urban associations. Representatives were concerned with protecting the rights of North Carolina Indians and providing services for them.

Initially, the NCCIA focused on education, housing, and employment. In recent years, the commission has included health-care concerns, as North Carolina Native Americans suffered from very high rates of diabetes, asthma, and heart disease. The NCCIA is one way in

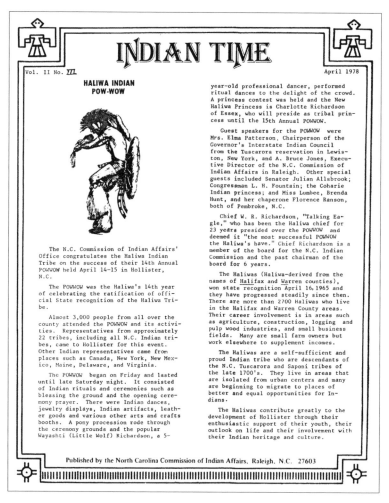

INDIAN TIME

Vol. II No. *III*   April 1978

HALIWA INDIAN POW-WOW

The N.C. Commission of Indian Affairs' Office congratulates the Haliwa Indian Tribe on the success of their 14th Annual POWWOW held April 14-15 in Hollister, N.C.

The POWWOW was the Haliwa's 14th year of celebrating the ratification of official State recognition of the Haliwa Tribe.

Almost 3,000 people from all over the county attended the POWWOW and its activities. Representatives from approximately 22 tribes, including all N.C. Indian tribes, came to Hollister for this event. Other Indian representatives came from places such as Canada, New York, New Mexico, Maine, Delaware, and Virginia.

The POWWOW began on Friday and lasted until late Saturday night. It consisted of Indian rituals and ceremonies such as blessing the ground and the opening ceremony prayer. There were Indian dances, jewelry displays, Indian artifacts, leather goods and various other arts and crafts booths. A pony procession rode through the ceremony grounds and the popular Wayashti (Little Wolf) Richardson, a 5-

year-old professional dancer, performed ritual dances to the delight of the crowd. A princess contest was held and the New Haliwa Princess is Charlotte Richardson of Essex, who will preside as tribal princess until the 15th Annual POWWOW.

Guest speakers for the POWWOW were Mrs. Elma Patterson, Chairperson of the Governor's Interstate Indian Council from the Tuscarora reservation in Lewiston, New York, and A. Bruce Jones, Executive Director of the N.C. Commission of Indian Affairs in Raleigh. Other special guests included Senator Julian Allsbrook; Congressman L. H. Fountain; the Coharie Indian princess; and Miss Lumbee, Brenda Hunt, and her chaperone Florence Ranson, both of Pembroke, N.C.

Chief W. R. Richardson, "Talking Eagle," who has been the Haliwa chief for 23 years presided over the POWWOW and deemed it "the most successful POWWOW the Haliwa's have." Chief Richardson is a member of the board for the N.C. Indian Commission and the past chairman of the board for 6 years.

The Haliwas (Haliwa-derived from the names of Halifax and Warren counties), won state recognition April 16, 1965 and they have progressed steadily since then. There are more than 2700 Haliwas who live in the Halifax and Warren County areas. Their career involvement is in areas such as agriculture, construction, logging and pulp wood industries, and small business fields. Many are small farm owners but work elsewhere to supplement incomes.

The Haliwas are a self-sufficient and proud Indian tribe who are descendants of the N.C. Tuscarora and Saponi tribes of the late 1700's. They live in areas that are isolated from urban centers and many are beginning to migrate to places of better and equal opportunities for Indians.

The Haliwas contribute greatly to the development of Hollister through their enthusiastic support of their youth, their outlook on life and their involvement with their Indian heritage and culture.

Published by the North Carolina Commission of Indian Affairs, Raleigh, N.C. 27603

The North Carolina Commission of Indian Affairs, established by the General Assembly in 1971, provides a variety of services to North Carolina's Indian community. The commission publishes *Indian Time*, a bimonthly newsletter, to inform North Carolina's Native Americans of current activities affecting Indian groups throughout the state.

which native Carolinians worked together to improve their lives. Recognizing that Indian people often faced similar problems elsewhere in the United States, some native Carolinians worked with Indians nationwide by joining groups such as the National Congress of American Indians, an organization committed to preserving native cultures and defending Indian rights.

In the early twenty-first century, the Eastern Band of Cherokee Indians remained the only tribe in North Carolina fully recognized by the United States government. Consequently, the Bureau of Indian Affairs (BIA) continued to provide services for the Cherokees. These services, which included schools and medical care, derived from a series of treaties and agreements between the federal government and the Cherokees that dated back to the nineteenth century. BIA services should not be considered handouts or welfare but rather what the Cherokees received in partial compensation for the thousands of acres of land they were forced to cede to the federal government. Today, the Cherokees have a tribal land base of about 55,000 acres, the title of which the federal government holds in trust. As a sovereign entity, the Cherokees govern themselves and their territory democratically. Cherokees may vote in elections for principal chief, vice chief, and a tribal council of twelve members, two from each township.

Unlike the Cherokees, other North Carolina Indians do not reside on reservations and are subject to state law. Furthermore, they have not benefitted from a tourist economy the way that the Cherokees have. Many Indians have traditionally been small farmers, and the economic changes in eastern North Carolina in the late twentieth century had a major impact on many American Indian communities in the state. In the late twentieth century, several of these communities, including the Lumbees, the Waccamaws, and the Coharies, formed economic development associations to help Indians apply for loans and grants with which to open businesses, offer managerial advice, operate daycare centers, find scholarships for students, renovate houses, and provide various services. The activities of the Waccamaw-Siouan Development Association, for example, ranged from attempting to locate industry in the community to building a community center. Private initiative helped as well. In the 1970s, a group of Lumbees founded the Lumbee Bank in Pembroke, the first Indian-owned bank in the United States. The bank provided loans as well as other financial services to individuals and businesses. After integration, some Indians looked to education to increase their economic opportunities. In the 1990s, an increasing number of young Native Americans took advantage of opportunities in higher education, and by the early twenty-first century, Pembroke and other Indian communities could boast of a growing number of Native American professionals in medicine, law, business, and academia. Despite some success, there were still serious economic problems in most Indian communities. In the early 2000s, approximately one-fifth of Native American families in North Carolina lived below the poverty line, and the unemployment rate for Indians was twice the state average.

Modern North Carolina Indian Communities and Organizations

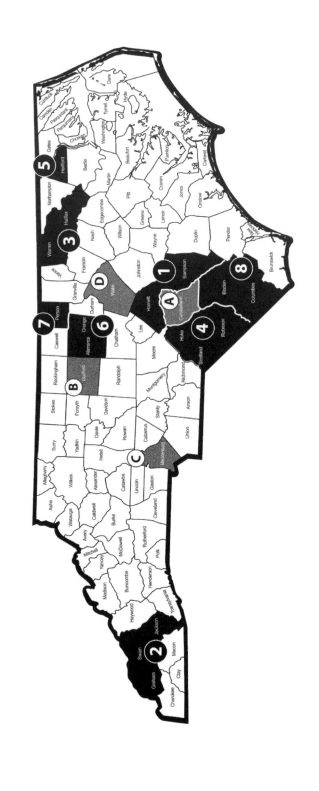

Communities

1 Coharies *(Harnett and Sampson)*

2 Eastern Band of Cherokee Indians *(Graham, Jackson, and Swain)*

3 Haliwa-Saponis *(Halifax and Warren)*

4 Lumbees *(Hoke, Robeson, and Scotland)*

5 Meherrins *(Hertford)*

6 Occaneechi Band of the Saponi Nation *(Alamance and Orange)*

7 Sapponis *(Person)*

8 Waccamaw-Siouans *(Bladen and Columbus)*

Organizations

Ⓐ Cumberland County Association for Indian People, Inc.

Ⓑ Guilford Native American Association, Inc.

Ⓒ Metrolina Native American Association, Inc.

Ⓓ Triangle Native American Society, Inc.

Courtesy of the Commission of Indian Affairs, http://www.doa.nc.gov/cia/resources.htm/FirstPeople-Brochure-08.pdf, adapted by Jayce Williams, 2010.

Because the other Native American tribes in North Carolina have surrendered land and endured years of oppression, they too are attempting to secure the services of the BIA; but budgetary concerns, technicalities, and bureaucratic indifference have made this difficult.

In the late twentieth century, Native Americans in North Carolina, like many others across the country, experienced a cultural revival. In communities across the state, American Indians made a concerted effort to preserve and celebrate their cultural traditions. They did so in two ways. First, Native Americans looked inward to protect their own cultural traditions unique to their communities, such as language, wood carving, beadwork, pottery, leatherwork, and other arts and crafts. For example, the Haliwa–Saponis received a federal grant to teach traditional arts and crafts to younger members of their community. Likewise, the Coharies and the Waccamaws introduced arts and crafts programs. In the Piedmont, Greensboro became a center for exhibiting and promoting Native American art. In the 1990s, the Greensboro Cultural Center founded the Guilford Native Amerian Art Gallery, which became an important venue for exhibiting the work of North Carolina Indian artists, such as C. M. Dreamweaver Cooper, Senora Lynch, and James Locklear. The remodeled Cherokee Museum on Qualla Boundary is also an important facility for the preservation and exhibition of Cherokee art and material culture.

North Carolina Indians also looked outward to broader pan-Indian cultural traditions. The most obvious manifestation of this second trend was the emergence of the modern powwow. The Haliwa-Saponis hosted the first contemporary powwow in North Carolina in 1967, which at the time was primarily a community celebration of internal Indian identity. Over the next two decades, the popularity of these events increased dramatically across the state. By the late 1990s, the annual powwow schedule, which ran from April to November, was practically full statewide, with various communities and organizations holding tribal and intertribal celebrations. Moreover, powwows evolved into external assertions of Indian identity, as well as internal celebrations, as powwows attracted thousands of visitors, including many non-Indians. Powwows also became economic ventures. Vendors sold a variety of Native American goods, including food, clothing, jewelry, pottery, books, and music. The center of the powwow, however, remained dancing. Native American dancers made their own outfits, or regalia. Younger Native Americans often preferred "fancy dancing," which was faster, more athletic, and required elaborate and colorful regalia. Traditional dances were typically slower, and the regalia often

These Native Americans gathered at the 24th annual Haliwa-Saponi Powwow in Hollister, N.C., in 1989, to celebrate the heritage of Indians of eastern North Carolina through dancing and drumming. Photographs reproduced with permission from the *News and Observer*.

mirrored nature. In recent years, contest powwows, where dancers compete for prizes, have become increasingly popular.

Indian tribes in North Carolina presently differ in their economic concerns, their tribal organizations, their relations with state and federal governments, and the extent to which their traditional languages and cultures have survived into the twenty-first century. Nevertheless, they share a pride in their heritage and in the contributions they have made to the state. The arrival of Europeans set in motion a tragic series of events that resulted in the destruction, dispossession, and oppression of native people. Indians have had to struggle to preserve their communities and to achieve equal rights and opportunities. While remembering the past, they presently look ahead to the future with pride in who they are and what they have achieved as citizens of the state and as native Carolinians.

APPENDIX

Important Dates in North Carolina Indian History
(Compiled by the North Carolina Commission of Indian Affairs)

ca. 40,000 B.C.E.	People migrate to North America by way of the Bering Land Bridge.
8000–1000 B.C.E.	Archaic tradition.
ca. 1200 B.C.E.	Southeastern Indians begin growing squash and gourds.
1000 B.C.E.–A.D. 700	Woodland tradition.
ca. 200 B.C.E.	Southeastern Indians begin cultivating corn.
A.D. 700–1500	Mississippian tradition.
1524	Italian navigator Giovanni da Verrazzano is the first European explorer to visit the Indians of North Carolina. He lands at Cape Fear and the Outer Banks.
1540	Hernando de Soto and his expedition visit Indian communities in western North Carolina on his march north from Florida.
1566	A Spanish expedition led by Juan Pardo visits the Catawba, Wateree, and Saxapahaw tribes of Carolina.
1584	Sir Walter Raleigh's first expedition visits the Indians of Roanoke Island.
1585	English colony is established at Roanoke Island under the direction of Sir Walter Raleigh. Colony fails the following year.
1587	John White's colony is established on Roanoke Island.

1590	Disappearance of John White's colony. Henceforth this colony is called the "Lost Colony."
1650	The beginning of a steady stream of white settlers moves into Indian lands along the coastal sounds and rivers of North Carolina.
1664	Clarendon County colony from Barbados is established in the Cape Fear region. Several years of Indian-white conflict ends the colony.
1670	German physician John Lederer visits the tribes of coastal North Carolina.
1675	The first Indian "war" in North Carolina erupts between the Chowan Indians and white settlers in Virginia.
1701–1711	Surveyor John Lawson visits the tribes of eastern North Carolina. He is killed by the Tuscaroras in 1711.
1711	Tuscarora War begins.
1713	Tuscarora War ends. The majority of the defeated Tuscaroras seek refuge with the Five Nations of the Iroquois in New York State.
1715	Peace treaty with remaining North Carolina Tuscaroras is signed. Tuscaroras, Corees, and Machapungas are placed on reservation established in Hyde County near Lake Mattamuskeet. By 1761 the reservation ceased to exist.
1730	Cherokee leaders visit London, confer with the king of England, and pledge eternal friendship to the British.
1732	Lumbee Henry Berry Lowry and James Lowry are granted land on the Lowry Swamp east of the Lumber River.
1738–1739	Smallpox epidemic ravages Indian population in North Carolina.

1755	Proposal to establish an Indian academy in present-day Sampson County is approved by the colonial governor.
1775	Cherokees cede large tract of land in central and western Kentucky, southwestern Virginia, and parts of north and northwestern Tennessee in the "Henderson Purchase."
1776	Cherokees side with the British during the American Revolution. The Coharies and Lumbees fight on the side of the Americans.
1785	Cherokees sign the Treaty of Hopewell, which delineates the boundaries of Cherokee territory.
1791	Cherokees sign the Treaty of Holston and are forced by treaty to cede 100-mile tract of land in exchange for goods and annuity of $1,000 per year.
1802	Cherokee National Council is established.
1808	Cherokees establish a law code and the "Light Horse Guards" to maintain law and order.
1810	Cherokees abolish clan revenge as a mechanism for social control.
1812–1814	Cherokees fight on the side of Americans to put down Tecumseh's efforts to drive out whites. Several Lumbees serve in American forces during the War of 1812.
1817	Cherokees cede land in exchange for land on the Arkansas River, and 2,000 Cherokees move west.
1820	Cherokees establish judicial administration and eight districts.
1821	Cherokee National Council approves the Cherokee Syllabary invented by Sequoya between 1809 and 1821.
1822	Cherokee National Supreme Court is established.

1825	New Cherokee capital is established at New Echota.
1827	Cherokees approve a new tribal constitution.
1828	First edition of the *Cherokee Phoenix*, a newspaper printed in Cherokee and English, is released.
1830	U.S. Congress passes Indian Removal Act.
1835	Cherokee Removal Treaty is signed.
1838–1839	Cherokees are removed to Oklahoma on the "Trail of Tears."
1840	North Carolina General Assembly passes law prohibiting Indians from owning or carrying weapons without first obtaining license.
1848	Catawbas at Cherokee request Bureau of Indian Affairs (BIA) to appoint an official to organize their removal to the West.
1862–1872	Lumbee Henry Berry Lowry and his triracial band wage "war" against the white establishment in Robeson County for injustices to Indians.
1868	New North Carolina Constitution, which restores voting rights to Indians, is passed.
1885	Indians in Robeson, Richmond, and Sampson counties are recognized as the "Croatan" by the North Carolina General Assembly. Legislation also provides for separate schools for the "Croatan."
1887	Croatan Normal School for the Indians of Robeson County is established one mile west of Pembroke and is given an appropriation of $500 by the North Carolina General Assembly.
1889	Eastern Band of Cherokee Indians is incorporated under North Carolina law.

1907	North Carolina General Assembly mandates separate schools for the "Croatan Indians and Creoles of Cumberland County."
1910	Coharies hold their first recorded community meeting and elect a tribal chief.
	Shiloh Indian School is constructed in Sampson County. Operating funds for the school are secured from a monthly fee charged each student. School closes in 1938.
1911	North Carolina General Assembly changes name of Croatans to "Indians of Robeson County."
	Croatan Normal School is renamed Indian Normal School of Robeson County.
	High Plains Indian School for the Indians of Person County is established. School closes in 1962.
	New Bethel Indian School is established for Indians in Sampson County. School closes in 1941.
1913	Indians of Robeson County are renamed "Cherokee Indians of Robeson County" by the North Carolina General Assembly.
	Indians living in Person County (formerly called "Cubans") are officially designated as "Indians of Person County" by the North Carolina General Assembly.
1925	Cherokee lands are placed in trust status with the federal government.
1933	Wide-Awake School for Waccamaw-Siouans is established in Columbus County. School closes in 1966.
1935	North Carolina General Assembly passes act to provide for the preservation of Indian antiquities in North Carolina. Citizens are "urged" to comply. No criminal penalties are set.

1937	North Carolina General Assembly empowers governor to set aside "some day" as "Indian Day."
1940	First college degree is granted at Indian Normal School of Robeson County.
1941	Name of Indian Normal School of Robeson County is changed by General Assembly to "Pembroke State College for Indians."
1942	East Carolina Indian School is established in Sampson County to serve Indians in seven surrounding counties. School closes in 1965.
1947	First Indian mayor of town of Pembroke is elected. Prior to this date, the governor of North Carolina appointed the mayors of Pembroke, all of whom were non-Indians.
1950	Funding of Cherokee Historical Association and first performance of outdoor drama *Unto These Hills*.
1952	Hawkeye Indian School for the Indians living in Hoke County is established. School closes in 1968.
1953	Lumbees (formerly called Cherokee Indians of Robeson County) are recognized by the state of North Carolina.
1954	Les Maxwell School for the Indians of Cumberland County is established. School closes in 1967.
1956	"Lumbee Bill" is passed by U.S. Congress. The bill recognizes the Lumbees as an Indian tribe but denies them services from the BIA.
1957	Haliwa Elementary and Secondary School is established. School closes in 1968.
1958	Lumbees successfully thwart attempt by Ku Klux Klan to establish itself in Robeson County.

1965	Haliwas receive state recognition as an Indian tribe.
1968	Lumbee Regional Development Association (LRDA) is chartered by the state of North Carolina.
1969	Pembroke State College for Indians becomes Pembroke State University and part of the University of North Carolina system.
1970	East Carolina Tuscarora Indian Association is established in Robeson County.
	Waccamaw-Siouan Development Association (WSDA) is chartered.
	Cherokee Civic Center is completed.
1971	Coharie and Waccamaw-Siouan tribes are recognized by the state of North Carolina.
	North Carolina Commission of Indian Affairs is established by the North Carolina General Assembly.
	First Indian-owned bank in the United States—Lumbee Bank—is chartered.
1973	*Carolina Indian Voice*, an Indian-owned newspaper, begins operation in Robeson County.
1973	Cumberland County Association for Indian People (CCAIP) is chartered.
	Henry Ward Oxendine, a Lumbee from Robeson County, becomes the first North Carolina-born Indian to serve in the North Carolina House of Representatives.
1974	Haliwa Tribe, Inc., is chartered.
1975	Guilford Native American Association (GNAA) and the Coharie Intra-Tribal Council are chartered.
	New multi-million-dollar Cherokee High School opens.

1976	Metrolina Native American Association (MNAA) is chartered.
1976	The outdoor drama *Strike at the Wind*, the story of Lumbee Henry Berry Lowry, opens in Robeson County.
1977	Meherrin Tribe is chartered by North Carolina.
1978	Bureau of Indian Affairs establishes procedure for federal acknowledgment of Native American tribes seeking recognition.
1980	Gov. James B. Hunt Jr. proclaims "Indian Heritage Week."
1981	Lumbees and Haliwas received membership in the National Congress of American Indians (NCAI).
	The "Unmarked Human Burial and Human Skeletal Remains Protection Act" and the "Archaeological Resources Protection Act" are unanimously passed by the North Carolina General Assembly. Criminal penalties are set for violations, and involvement of Indian communities is mandated in decisions concerning treatment, analysis, and disposition of Native American remains.
1985	Eno-Occaneechi Tribe is chartered by North Carolina.
1986	Meherrin Tribe is recognized by North Carolina.
1988	U.S. Congress passes the Indian Gaming Regulatory Act.
	Two Robeson County Native Americans hold hostages in the office of the local newspaper to draw attention to corruption in the county.
1994	Eastern Band of Cherokee Indians signs gaming compact with North Carolina.
1997	Harrah's Cherokee Casino opens in Cherokee.

1997	The North Carolina General Assembly passes a resolution restoring recognition to the Indians of Person County, now known as the Sapponis.
	Eastern Band of Cherokee Indians buys Kituwah Mound.
2000	The North Carolina Commission of Indian Affairs recognizes the Triangle Native American Society.
	Lorna McNeill (Lumbee) is crowned Miss North Carolina.
2002	Occaneechi Band of the Saponi Nation is recognized by North Carolina.
2005	Governor Michael Easley signs a bill designating the University of North Carolina, Pembroke as the state's historically Indian university.
2009	U.S. House passes bill to recognize Lumbee Indians (bill moved to Senate for consideration).

SOURCES AND SUGGESTED READING

A number of works have been written about North Carolina Indians, including an earlier publication by the North Carolina Division (now Office) of Archives and History, Stanley A. South's *Indians in North Carolina* (Raleigh, 1959), now out of print. Others include Douglas Le Tell Rights, *The American Indian in North Carolina* (Durham: Duke University Press, 1947; reprinted, Winston-Salem: John F. Blair, 1957), and Ruth Y. Wetmore, *First on the Land: The North Carolina Indians* (Winston-Salem: John F. Blair, 1975). Teachers, in particular, will find much valuable information in Rachael Bonny, *Ethnic Studies Guide and Resource Manual for the Carolinas* (Charlotte: University of North Carolina at Charlotte, 1978). A useful pamphlet, *North Carolina Indians*, has been published by the North Carolina Commission of Indian Affairs. The commission also issues a newspaper entitled *Indian Time*. Other newspapers of interest are the *Carolina Indian Voice*, published in Robeson County, and the *Cherokee One Feather* (Cherokee, North Carolina).

CHAPTER 1: NATIVE AMERICA

For additional information on North Carolina prehistory and archaeology, see Mark A. Mathis and Jeffrey J. Crow, eds., *The Prehistory of North Carolina: An Archaeological Symposium* (Raleigh: Division of Archives and History, Department of Cultural Resources, 1983); Joffre Lanning Coe, "The Cultural Sequence of the Carolina Piedmont," in *Archaeology of the Eastern United States*, edited by James B. Griffin (Chicago: University of Chicago Press, 1952); Roy S. Dickens Jr., *Cherokee Prehistory: The Pisgah Phase in the Appalachian Summit Region* (Knoxville: University of Tennessee Press, 1976); James B. Griffin, "Eastern North American Archaeology: A Summary," *Science*, 156 (April 14, 1967), 175-191; Bennie C. Keel, *Cherokee Archaeology: A Study of the Appalachian Summit* (Knoxville: University of Tennessee Press, 1976); and H. Trawick Ward and R. P. Stephen Davis Jr., *Time before History: The Archaeology of North Carolina* (Chapel Hill: University of North Carolina Press, 1999). For children or general readers, Roy S. Dickens Jr. and James L. McKinley's *Frontiers in the Soil* (Atlanta: Frontiers Publishing Company, 1979) is highly recommended.

CHAPTER 2: THE INDIAN WAY OF LIFE

A collection of early observations of Native Carolinians can be found in David Leroy Corbitt, *Explorations, Descriptions, and Attempted Settlements of Carolina, 1584–1590* (Raleigh: State Department of Archives and History, 1948). Other good accounts are Robbie Ethridge and Charles Hudson, ed. *The Transformation of the Southeastern Indians 1540–1760* (Jackson: University Press of Mississippi, 2002); David B. Quinn and Alison M. Quinn, *The First Colonists: Documents on the Planting of the First English Settlements in North America, 1584–1590* (Raleigh: Division of Archives and History, North Carolina Department of Cultural Resources, 1982); John Lawson, *A New Voyage to Carolina*, edited by Hugh Talmage Lefler (Chapel Hill: University of North Carolina Press, 1967; reprinted 1984); and James Adair, *Adair's History of the American Indian*, edited by Samuel Cole Williams (Johnson City, Tenn.: Watauga Press, 1930). Charles Hudson's *The Southeastern Indians* (Knoxville: University of Tennessee Press, 1976) and Gregory A. Waselkov, *Powhatan's Mantle: Indians in the Colonial Southeast* (Lincoln: University of Nebraska Press, 2006) are excellent studies of native cultures. A good book for young readers is Jesse Burt and Robert Ferguson's *Indians of the Southeast: Then and Now* (Nashville and New York: Abingdon Press, 1973).

CHAPTER 3: INDIAN-WHITE RELATIONS

Two books on early Indian-white relations are J. Leitch Wright Jr., *The Only Land They Knew: The Tragic Story of the American Indians in the Old South* (New York: Free Press, 1981), and Elizabeth Fenn and Peter Wood, *Natives and Newcomers: The Way We Lived in North Carolina before 1770* (Chapel Hill: University of North Carolina Press, 1983). Works on the Indian trade include Verner Winslow Crane, *The Southern Frontier, 1670–1732* (Durham: Duke University Press, 1928), and John Phillip Reid, *A Better Kind of Hatchet: Law, Trade, and Diplomacy in the Cherokee Nation during the Early Years of European Contact* (University Park, Pa.: Pennsylvania State University, 1976). E. Lawrence Lee's *Indian Wars in North Carolina, 1663–1763* (Raleigh: Carolina Charter Tercentenary Commission, 1963; reprinted, Raleigh: State Department of Archives and History, 1968) is a useful survey. For additional information on the Tuscarora War, see Douglas W. Boyce, "Did a Tuscarora Confederacy Exist?" in *Four Centuries of Southern Indians*, edited by Charles M. Hudson (Athens: University of Georgia Press, 1978), and Thomas C. Parramore, "The Tuscarora Ascendancy," *North Carolina Historical Review* 59 (October 1982), 307-326. Additional information on Cherokee alliances and enmity can be found in David H. Corkran, *The Cherokee Frontier: Conflict and Survival, 1740–62* (Norman: University of Oklahoma Press, 1962); John R. Alden, *John Stuart and The Southern Colonial Frontier, 1754–1775* (Ann Arbor: University of Michigan Press, 1944); and James H. O'Donnell III, *The Cherokees of North Carolina in the American Revolution* (Raleigh: Division of Archives and History, Department of Cultural Resources, 1976). Other valuable resources include: Kirsten Fischer, *Sex, Race, and Resistance in Colonial North Carolina* (Ithaca: Cornell University Press, 2001); Charles Hudson, *The Juan Pardo Expeditions: Spanish Explorers and the Indians of the Carolinas and Tennessee, 1566–1568* (Washington, D.C.: Smithsonian Institution Press, 1990); Noeleen McIlvenna, *A Very Mutinous People: The Struggle for North Carolina, 1660–1713* (Chapel Hill: University of North Carolina Press, 2009); and William G. McLoughlin, *Cherokee Renascence in the New Republic* (Princeton: Princeton University Press, 1986).

CHAPTER 4: THE CHEROKEES

Among the many works on Cherokee history are the following: Heidi M. Altman, *Eastern Cherokee Fishing* (Tuscaloosa: University of Alabama Press, 2006); Christina Taylor Beard-Moose, *Public Indians, Private Cherokees: Tourism and Tradition on Tribal Ground* (Tuscaloosa: University of Alabama Press, 2009); John R. Finger, *Cherokee Americans: The Eastern Band of Cherokees in the Twentieth Century* (Lincoln: University of Nebraska Press, 1984); Sarah H. Hill, *Weaving New Worlds: Southeastern Cherokee Women and Their Basketry* (Chapel Hill: University of North Carolina Press, 1997); Izumi Ishii, *Bad Fruits of the Civilized Tree: Alcohol & the Sovereignty of the Cherokee Nation* (Lincoln: University of Nebraska Press, 2008); Duane H. King, ed., *The Cherokee Indian Nation: A Troubled History* (Knoxville: University of Tennessee Press, 1979); Henry T. Malone, *Cherokees of the Old South: A People in Transition* (Athens: University of Georgia Press, 1956); Sharlotte Neely, *Snowbird Cherokees: People of Persistence* (Athens: University of Georgia Press, 1991); Theda Perdue, *Cherokee*

Women: Gender and Culture Change, 1700–1835 (Lincoln: University of Nebraska Press, 1998); Theda Perdue, *Slavery and the Evolution of Cherokee Society, 1540–1866* (Knoxville: University of Tennessee Press, 1979); Theda Perdue and Michael D. Green, *The Cherokee Nation and the Trail of Tears* (New York: Penguin Library of American Indian History, 2007); and Grace Steele Woodward, *The Cherokees* (Norman: University of Oklahoma Press, 1963). The Cherokees of North Carolina are the subject of John R. Finger, *The Eastern Band of Cherokees, 1819–1900* (Knoxville: University of Tennessee Press, 1984). Recommended for young readers are Glen Fleischman, *The Cherokee Removal, 1838* (New York: Franklin Watts, 1971), and Peter Collier, *When Shall They Rest? The Cherokee's Long Struggle with America* (New York: Holt, Rinehart, and Winston, 1973).

CHAPTER 5: THE LUMBEES

Scholarly works on the Lumbees include Karen I. Blu, *The Lumbee Problem: The Making of an American Indian People* (Cambridge and New York: Cambridge University Press, 1980; reprinted, Lincoln: University of Nebraska Press, 2001); Adolph L. Dial, *The Lumbee* (New York: Chelsea House, 1993); Adolph L. Dial and David K. Eliades, *The Only Land I Know: A History of the Lumbee Indians* (San Francisco: Indian Historian Press, 1975); David K. Elides and Linda Oxendine, *Pembroke State University: A History* (Columbus, Ga.: Brentwood University Press, 1986); William McKee Evans, *To Die Game: The Story of the Lowry Band, Indian Guerrillas of Reconstruction* (Baton Rouge: Louisiana State University Press, 1971); Malinda Maynor Lowery, *Lumbee Indians in the Jim Crow South: Race, Identity, and the Making of a Nation* (Chapel Hill: University of North Carolina Press, 2010); Gerald Sider, *Living Indian Histories: Lumbee and Tuscarora People in North Carolina* (Chapel Hill: University of North Carolina Press, 2003); Glenn Ellen Starr, *The Lumbee Indians: An Annotated Bibliography, with Chronology and Index* (Jefferson, N.C.: McFarland & Company, Inc., 1994); and Walt Wolfram, Clare Danneberg, Stanley Knick, and Linda Oxendine, *Fine in the World: Lumbee Language in Time and Place* (Raleigh: North Carolina State University, 2002).

CHAPTER 6: NATIVE CAROLINIANS TODAY

Contemporary Indian problems are dealt with in Patricia Lerch, *Waccamaw Legacy: Contemporary Indians Fight for Survival* (Tuscaloosa: The University of Alabama Press, 2004); Christopher Arris Oakley, *Keeping the Circle: American Indian Identity in Eastern North Carolina, 1885–2004* (Lincoln: University of Nebraska Press, 2005); and Susan M. Presti, ed., *Public Policy and Native Americans in North Carolina: Issues for the '80s* (Raleigh: North Carolina Center for Public Policy Research, 1981). Reporter Gary Dorsey contributed a series of revealing articles to the *Sentinel* (Winston-Salem) between April 27 and May 5, 1981. The Lumbees are one of the tribes whose situation is examined in *Report on Terminated and Nonfederally Recognized Indians: Final Report to the American Indian Policy Review Commission* (Washington, D.C.: Government Printing Office, 1976). The following articles, which appear in Walter L. Williams, ed., *Southeastern Indians since the Removal Era* (Athens: University of Georgia Press, 1979), concern North Carolina Indians: Sharlotte Neely, "Acculturation and Persistence among North Carolina's Eastern Band of Cherokee Indians," and W. McKee Evans, "The North Carolina Lumbees: From Assimilation to Revitalization." Although dated, John Gulick's *Cherokees at the Crossroads* (Chapel Hill: University of North Carolina Press, 1960; revised edition, 1973) is still useful. Another valuable resource is Thomas Ross, *American Indians in North Carolina: Geographic Interpretations* (Southern Pines, N.C.: Kara Hollow Press, 1999).

INDEX

Employment, 51, 66, 67

English (people): alliance with, 32; built forts, 36; dominated coastal Carolina tribes, 36; education, 41, 42; establish colony at Roanoke Island, 75; Lumbees adopted ways of, 53; retaliated, 29; settlements, 38; trade with, 22

English (language): and Cherokee newspaper, 78; and Lumbees, 53; missionaries forced Indian children to speak, 45; speaking, seen as sign of civilization, 40

Eno-Occaneechi (tribe), 82

Enos (tribe), 22, 28

Epidemic(s), 27, 38, 53, 76

Ethnicity: loss of, 64, 65; preservation of, 53, 58, 63

Ethnocentricity, 14, 29, 60

Euchella (Cherokee leader), 45

European(s): arrival of, 11, 14, 17, 26, 29, 73; culture, 14, 16, 40; Indian contact with, 27, 28, 31; manufactured goods, 27, pictured, 29; settlers, 13, 17, 33, 53, 63; trade with, 29, 30

Excavations, 2, 3; pictured, 5

F

Family/families, 40, 65; Cherokee, 44; Chowan, 34; lived below poverty line, 49, 69; pictured, 48, 67; relationships within, 16, 20

Farmers, 3, 40, 69

Farm(s)/farming: changing economy of, 66; Indians made living through, 17, 65; Lumbees and, 53, 55; Mississippian people and, 11; pictured, 47; pioneer, 40; scientific techniques for, 46

Fayetteville, N.C., 66

Federal Acknowledgment Process (FAP), 62

Federal government. See Government; United States government

Federal recognition. See Recognition, federal

Fire(s), 9, 18, 20, 21, 22, 64

Fish/fishing, 6, 11, 17, 20, 22

Five Nations of the Iroquois, 76

Florence, S.C., 54

Florida, 36, 74

Food: of Archaic peoples, 7; destruction of, 17, 40; methods of procuring, 4, 18, 20, 39; provision of, 22, 27; seized, 55–56, 57; sources of, 6, 11, 18, 20; and Woodland people, 9. See also Corn; Crop(s); Nuts; Seeds; Squash

Fort Dobbs, 36

Fort Hancock, 33

Fort Loudoun, 36, 38

Fort Narhantes, 33

Fort Neoheroka, 34

Fort Prince George, 36; map of, pictured, 37

Forts. See by name

Franklin, N.C., 38

French, 36, 38

French and Indian War, 38

G

Gambling, 52

Game (animals), 5, 6, 7, 17, 44. See also Animal(s)

Gaming: and Cherokees, 50, 51, 82

Gathering, 17; wild food, 4, 20, 39

General Assembly. See North Carolina General Assembly

Georgia, 12, 43; Cherokees in, 36, 41, 42, 44

German, 33, 76

Gourd(s), 22, 24, 75; pictured, 19

Government: and Cherokee lands, 79; of Indians varied widely, 16, 22; seized native property, 66. See also Colonial government/officials; United States government

Governor, 80. See also by name

Graffenried, Baron Christoph von, 33; capture of, pictured, 34

Graham County, N.C., 70–71

Grant, Col. James, 38

Granville, Lord, 35

Great Depression, 46

Great Smoky Mountains National Park, 48

Green Corn Ceremony, 17

Greensboro, N.C., 66, 72

Greensboro Cultural Center, 72

Pembroke State University, 58, 81

Person County, 65; Indian communities in, 63, 70–71; Indian family in, pictured, 67; Indians in, recognized by N.C. General Assembly, 83

Petitions, 44, 62, 65

Piedmont: burials in, 10–11; center for exhibiting/promoting Native American art, 72; European settlement in, 63; evidence of Paleo-Indians in, 5; excavation project in, pictured, 3; explored by John Lawson, 15; invaded by Mississippians, 11; Siouan-speaking tribes occupied, 14; Woodland people in, 9

Pits, 2, 3, 9; used for burial, 10, 11

Plantations, 31, 41, 55

Planter(s), 53, 56; prominent, 30, 42, 43; in Robeson County, 54, 55

Points, 3, 6, 9, 10; projectile, pictured, 5

Political organization: and Cherokess, 42; contributed to unity, 14; Indians bargained with, 58, 60; and Lumbees, 62; and Mississippians, 11

Politics: and Indian anxiety, 33; and Lumbees, 60; and public services for Indians, 58; Republican Party dominated N.C., 56

Pomeiock (Indian village): pictured, 21

Population (Indian), 6, 75

Pottery, 3, 7, 9, 11, 21, 48, 72; pictured, 7, 10

Poverty, 34, 49, 69

Powwow, 72; pictured, 73

President of the United States, 44, 51. *See also by individual name*

Prisoners: Cherokee, 37, 45; tortured, 26

Projectile points: pictured, 5

Property: community, 29; protection of, 42; rights, 35; seized by government, 66; taxes, 45

Prospect School: pictured, 59

Q

Quakers, 45

Qualla Arts and Crafts cooperative, 48

Qualla Boundary: and Cherokee land purchase, 45; and Cherokee Museum, 72; economy of, 49, 51; and Harrah's Cherokee Casino, 50, 51; national park adjoining, 48

R

Race: bias over, 60, 61, 62, 64; differences in, 16; equality of, 62; hiring based on, 61; integration by, 65; nonwhites considered inferior, 58; segregation by, 58, 60, 63

Radical Republicans, 56

Raids, 54, 55, 57

Raleigh, Sir Walter, 12, 29, 58, 75

Raleigh, N.C., 66, 67

Reagan, [President Ronald], 49

Recognition of Indian tribes: federal, 62, 68-69; state, 66

Reconstruction, 56, 58

Religion, 11, 16

Republican Party, 56

Revolution, American. *See* American Revolution

Richmond County, N.C., 78

River(s), 27, 38, 53; settlements near, 11, 12, 14, 22, 33, 36, 53. *See also* Stream(s) *and by name*

Roanoke Island, 12, 75

Roanoke River, 33, 34

Robeson County, N.C.: Croatans in, 78; and "double voting," 60; East Carolina Tuscarora Indian Association established in, 81; Indian communities in, 70–71; and Ku Klux Klan, 61, 80; Lumbees in, 53, 54, 57, 62, 63; segregation in, 58; Tuscaroras in, 63

Robeson County Courthouse, 54

Robesonian (newspaper), 61, 82

Ross, John (Cherokee chief), 42, 44; pictured, 43

Rutherford, Gen. Griffith, 39

S

Sampson County, N.C., 65; Croatans, in, 78; Indian communities in, 63, 70–71; schools established in, 76, 79, 80

Saponis (tribe), 28

Y